Praise for *Family Business Abundance*

"Brad Fisher and his Scalability process made a real difference at our company. Our infrastructure is now fully scalable, and our leadership team has reached a whole new level of alignment and capacity. We are growing at a quick pace, and thankfully, that growth is easier to manage."

Vince Bussio, founder and CEO, Armorock Polymer Concrete

"Brad had been instrumental in helping our business overcome issues that can come with running a family business. He also helped us achieve a level of service that matched our vision when we started our business. It has been a pleasure working with Brad and I am so grateful for the difference he has made for us."

Susan Bell, cofounder and board member,
James Mason Centers for Recovery

"For the past two years, I have had the privilege of working with Brad in our five-year-old family business. I have seen his commitment, knowledge and experience in action as we have benefited from the principles he outlines in his book. Understanding these principles will help anyone strengthen their family and business far into the future."

Michael Dobson, cofounder and board member,
James Mason Centers for Recovery

"Brad assisted our family in breaking down many false beliefs and misunderstandings that were impacting the ability of our business to operate effectively. During his time with us, Brad was able to completely transform our organization and management into a company with a strong leadership team who were empowered decision makers and had a passion for the work they were involved in. Thank you, Brad, for all you have done for us."

Paul Dobson, cofounder and board member,
James Mason Centers for Recovery

"*Brad Fisher's fine book offers a way for a family business to evoke and define its vision and mission and then to employ multiple practices to enable it to bring them to life. Kind of a McKinsey consulting book for family business. Highly practical and useful.*"

James E. Hughes, Jr., author of *Family Wealth Keeping it in the Family*; *Family: the Compact Among Generations*; coauthor with Susan Massenzio and Keith Whitaker of *Complete Family Wealth* and coauthor with Hartley Goldstone and Keith Whitaker of *Family Trusts*

"*Everyone with a family business is searching for tools and practices to sustain it and thrive across generations. Because they are a family before they are a business, this is more than a business issue. Success starts with yourself—as a business owner or member of a business family. This book is about the mindset and practices that you can use to help a family business, even one that is already successful, to grow and thrive in desired and also unexpected ways. Every page and every chapter is useful and invites the reader to respond immediately in useful ways.*"

Dennis Jaffe, author of *Borrowed from Your Grandchildren* and research associate at Wise Counsel Research

"*Families and Business. The importance of both is immense. Mixing family and business purposefully is challenging. Brad Fisher offers powerful, but easy to read and apply, suggestions on how we can avoid the "shirtsleeves to shirtsleeves in three generations" proverb. Family Business Abundance is a must read for family leaders and advisors who are deeply committed to the sustainability of both family and business.*"

John A. Warnick, founder and CEO of the Purposeful Planning Institute

"Clear, encouraging, and realistic, Family Business Abundance lays out a step-by-step path to success for family businesses. While the business industry preaches grow-to-sell, Fisher encourages families to grow-to-thrive across generations. By harnessing critical building blocks of engagement, clarity, and scalability, Fisher demonstrates how any business-owning family can generate wealth, engage their human capital–and, together, change the world."

Amelia Renkert-Thomas, author of *Engaged Ownership: A Guide for Owners of Family Businesses*

"Brad uses stories to frame constructive prescriptions for family business owners. From the first page, readers will discover the material is relevant and accessible as its sprinkled with dollops of personal digressions that make points come alive in the voice of a modest boy from North Dakota who has lived what he preaches."

Jamie McLaughlin, CEO, James H. McLaughlin & Co.

FAMILY
BUSINESS
ABUNDANCE

HOW TO SCALE YOUR COMPANY
AND SUCCEED TOGETHER ACROSS
MULTIPLE GENERATIONS

Bradley G. Fisher

INDIE BOOKS
INTERNATIONAL®

ISBN: 978-1-952233-20-3
Library of Congress Control Number: 2020915388

Family Business Management System™ is a pending trademark of Bradley G. Fisher.

Scalability RoadMap™ is a pending trademark of Bradley G. Fisher.

Family Business Growth Engine™ is a pending trademark of Bradley G. Fisher.

The use of the family business names and logos of Ford, Target, SC Johnson, Corning, Schilling, Rand McNally, Hallmark, Doubleday, Kendall-Jackson, Fidelity Investments, Andersen, and Campbells are the property of the respective companies are cited for educational purposes only, and the use of their company names does not imply endorsement of these companies for this book or the work of Bradley G. Fisher.

Designed by Joni McPherson, mcphersongraphics.com

INDIE BOOKS INTERNATIONAL, INC®
2424 VISTA WAY, SUITE 316
OCEANSIDE, CA 92054

www.indiebooksintl.com

To Kim, the boys, and EMF

TABLE OF CONTENTS

CHAPTER 1

Your Family Business Journey

T hank you for joining us on the path to long-term family business abundance. This journey may extend beyond your lifetime. But don't let that stop you. If you see your part through, the rewards for you and your family will be immense.

Powerful families have gone before us, big and small; families have been succeeding together for thousands of years, and they do so to this day. You need vision, strength, and courage to join them, and you will judge for yourself, nearly every day, whether the climb is worth the view.

We believe it *is*.

We believe that for the right people, family business is the best way to become wealthy, to cultivate human capacity, and to make an impact on the world. It can be incredibly satisfying, and at times, even fun to work with the ones whom you love the most.

Rewarding, satisfying, and sometimes even fun. But not *easy*.

Your aspirations, your family, and your business. Few things in life are more important. Family business provides the opportunity for you to integrate all three. And if you set the proper foundation in place, you can generate abundance for a hundred years or more.

Do you want to build a successful, multi-generational family business? If so, this book is for you, for the people with you today, and for future leaders, yet unborn, who will carry on your mission with purpose and gratitude in their hearts.

There are two core assertions in this book:

> Over the long-term, family business is the most rewarding path you can take. If you approach it right, you and your family can thrive together across multiple generations.
>
> The natural state for a well-tuned business is to grow. You can achieve natural growth and sustainable profit by building scalability into your organization.

This book is about how to *lean in*. How to make a family business *work*. Why it's *worth it*, how to make it *grow,* and how to make it *flourish*. Because when they succeed, family businesses generate long-term abundance.

Consider this a lifeboat for family business owners. If you resonate with our core message, or even if you're simply curious, then welcome aboard.

This book isn't for everyone, and it isn't meant to be.

Most business owners consider their companies a means to an end, a career choice, a gateway to status and respect. They intend to make a good living and then sell their businesses someday. Cash out. Achieve their *liquidity event*.

That is a fine perspective. It's all-American, a cornerstone of the economy.

Most family members share a similar perspective. They're aware of the company, of course; it is part of their lives, an element of their identities. But for them, it's a means to an end as well, someone else's business. The company belongs to their mother, their father, or their grandparents, but not to *them*; it's related, of course, but separate from their future lives and careers.

If your goal is to sell your business or pursue a different career, we applaud you. In fact, we believe every owner should run his or her business so it is ready to be sold at any time, optimized for the best price and the most positive legacy. If you're thinking about selling your company please continue reading, because you will improve your chance to achieve a successful transition. The chapters on clarity and scalability will prove especially helpful as you grow your company prior to sale.

However, please keep your mind open, and be aware that social pressure may be influencing your perspective. Today's culture, led by the media and countless pundits, expects and encourages business owners to *get out*. Sometimes it seems like you can't even boot up your phone without encountering an article, an ad, or an email that yells at you to *sell*. It's almost as if retirement, going out to pasture, is the only option we have.

Consider the lawyers, the accountants, the valuation experts, the investment bankers and business brokers who are hungry for their next transaction.

Entire industries exist to help us sell.

What about the wealth managers, eager to invest the proceeds of our liquidity event? What about the private equity firms who want to control what we have, pay the lowest possible price, and then benefit from the profits and growth we might have achieved on our own?

Come now. Let's be fair; please don't get me wrong. There are many wonderful advisors and private equity professionals out there. Many are our friends, and some of them are reading this book right now. If you're in this game for the right reasons, you should be proud of the value you bring to the world. We mean no disrespect, and we love collaborating with you.

There is a right time for everything, including the sale of your business. But be thoughtful, take your time, and manage the process carefully. If you play your cards right, you will achieve a much higher price. You will avoid unnecessary taxes, and you will enjoy much more satisfaction down the road.

And by the way, when you *do* sell, you can reinvest the proceeds into other ventures that will perpetuate your success across multiple generations.

This book provides an alternative to the conventional point of view, a voice in the wilderness, for those of us who want to remain entrepreneurial, who intend to build family business growth engines that can enable us to thrive together across multiple generations.

By the way, the "*we*" in this book refers to a small group of us, growing by the day, who belong to the Featherstone firm and tribe. We are entrepreneurs, business owners, family members, advisors, and friends who believe that the family business journey is worth all the effort. We are intrigued by the notion of a Hundred-Year Family, and some of us aim to make it happen. When you read the word "*we*" in that context, feel free to consider yourself one of us—or not. Your choice.

Consider these numbers:

100 years, 100 people, $100 million

Totally doable. It has a nice ring to it, does it not?

One hundred years? Think about that. Imagine the relationships you could build in that amount of time, the experiences you could share, the wealth you could accumulate, the impact your family could have on the world.

One hundred people? Certainly. Given five or six generations, it is entirely reasonable to assume that your family and your roster of key executives will expand to include at least that many folks, perhaps substantially more.

One hundred million dollars? That is a *no-brainer*. If you, your current team, and your descendants work it right, the math indicates far more than that. We will do that math together in a bit. Meanwhile, remember these numbers:

100, 100, $100 million

What do you ultimately want for your family, for your company, and for yourself?

This book presents a *management system* for family business, a set of concepts, tools, and techniques that can help you strengthen your family and your company, so you can build and sustain both across multiple generations.

On the surface, the *Family Business Management System* is simple. It consists of three *mindsets* and three *building blocks*. The mindsets will give you the perspective you need to focus your attention and sustain your conviction when the challenges get tough. The building blocks provide concrete guidelines and techniques you can use to create a sustainable foundation for your family and your business. We will devote a chapter or two to each.

Mindsets:	Building Blocks:
1. *Family Business Abundance*	1. *Engagement*
2. *Family Business vs. Family-owned Business*	2. *Clarity*
3. *Family Business Growth Engine*	3. *Scalability*

As our friend Mark LeBlanc would say, "What you need to know, and what you need to do."

A quick note about *stories*. Every family and individual has one, and so does every business, including yours. Some of the stories inspire us; others sound a warning call. Some are deceptively simple, while others weave complex tapestries across continents and centuries.

This book is filled with stories, all essentially true, but we owe our friends and clients the debt of confidentiality, so we've disguised and intertwined most of them.

What is the story behind *your* company? Did you launch it yourself? Perhaps someone passed it to you across a generation or two. How does your business saga blend with your family story, with your personal tale? Where is the drama, the pain, the conflict? How about the joy, the collaboration and payoff?

How will *your* story play out, one hundred years from now? Are you up for it?

Perhaps you're not interested in an extended time frame. Rather, you may be focused on the here and now. That's fine. You can employ the building blocks to double the size of your business, while increasing your profitability and enhancing your quality. The management system will enable you to achieve a higher valuation and take-out price, when you decide to sell your business.

If you *do* decide to build and share an enterprise with your family, one that lasts across multiple generations, how can you stack the deck in your favor?

In this book, we will explore each of these questions. Then we will show you how to develop a *Scalability RoadMap* you can use to guide your progress.

Successful multi-generational family businesses are rare, but with the right perspective and tools, yours can be one of them.

Personal Note—*Your Guide*

I am committed to this work. It brings me great joy. This may or may not become apparent to you as the book plays out, but that's not important. This book is not about *me*. I'm not interested in a book like that, and neither are you. This book is about *you*. About you and your *family*.

Think of me as your river guide, much like a veteran you would hire to run the Colorado river. You could travel it by yourself, of course, but you would expose yourself to dangers and delays—rocks, rapids, waterfalls, poison ivy, mountain lions—that you may not wish to handle on your own. At best, heading down alone would take too long, and at worst, your raft could capsize, causing you to lose everything.

I have been navigating family business waterways for decades. I don't claim to know every rock, bend, and pool, but I've paid attention along the way. I've survived steep, narrow passages, led many companies, worked with wonderful people, and learned *so* many lessons.

Some of the perceptions I gained the hard way might streamline *your* challenge, so you and I will set aside a bit of space at the end of most chapters. Sub-sections like these, brief messages, from me to you, followed by thought exercises, designed to lock it in.

These are thought exercises, so relax. I won't ask you to pull out a notebook. It usually rubs me the wrong way when authors do that, and besides, most readers don't comply even if you ask them to. If you *do* feel inclined to write a few things down as we go on, please go ahead. You'll get more out of the exercises than the people who don't.

By the way, Albert Einstein loved thought exercises. He would close his eyes and revel in them for hours at a time, which is often how he encountered his groundbreaking insights. I am no Einstein, and neither are you, but it's fun to know he would approve.

FOOD FOR THOUGHT EXERCISE – YOUR PERSONAL JOURNEY

Whether we like it or not, we all belong to a family, and the *notion* of family is crucial to our discussion. But make no mistake; this book is about *you*. No matter what generation you belong to, no matter how functional or crazy your family is today, no matter what stage of development your business is in, this book is for you. We are here to help you understand what is *possible*, to help you decide how you want to *fit in*, and where you want to go.

We are at the headwaters now, you and I, pushing off from shore. Before the current catches us, before we pick up speed, please take a moment to consider the journey itself. Think about where you are today and try to visualize your destination.

What are you afraid of? Where do you wish to *go*?

Close your eyes and *imagine* the journey. Give it a few minutes of reflection. The scene is foggy, I suppose. But don't worry. The air will clear as we proceed.

I hope life is good for you today. Not perfect, perhaps, but a fine place to start. You're facing a problem, though, or you wouldn't be reading this. Perhaps it's an aspiration you're burning to achieve, an obstacle you need to overcome, something you hope to learn, or a conflict you wish to resolve. What is it? What do you want from this book, and from your journey?

Your motivations will reveal themselves soon enough. For now, please know that we have a *plan*. As we drift through these pages, you will refine your destination, and together, we will harness a system to engage your family, clarify your circumstances, and achieve multi-generational success.

You are the hero of this movie. But remember, it's not a solo, lone-wolf feature. Your family is right there with you.

A Brief Overview: The Family Business Management System

I n this book, we introduce a comprehensive *management system* you can employ to strengthen your family and your business. The system consists of three *mindsets*, and three *building blocks*. Here are a diagram and brief previews of each:

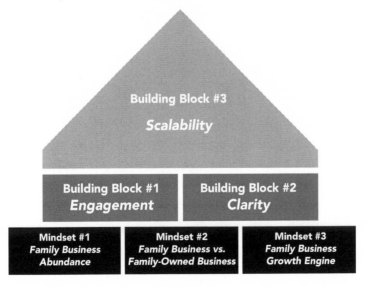

Please Note: This section provides simple summaries and lists. Each of the Mindsets and Building Blocks will have at least one chapter of its own, and there we will dig into each of the underlying lists in more detail.

MINDSET #1: Family Business Abundance

Family wealth extends far beyond cars, homes, and bank balances. Our culture tends to focus attention on the money and other assets, but family business provides so much more.

The concept of *family business abundance* asserts that if done right, your business will generate substantial *human capital*, *social capital*, *enterprise capital*, and *financial capital*, a profusion of wealth that can span across multiple generations.

Many families experience the world through a lens of *scarcity*, not abundance. This is fear-based thinking, a perspective that views life mostly as a series of compromises, restricted resources, threats from ambiguity, and unrealized dreams. This is not entirely off base, of course; life *is* filled with trade-offs, but when feelings of scarcity dominate a family's collective psyche, sad outcomes often result.

The perspective of abundance is far more rewarding. Families who view life through a lens of abundance experience many benefits, and some of those families sustain abundance for a hundred years or more. These people never have perfect days either; none of us do. Nothing is ever perfect. But if you embrace a mindset of abundance, it is likely to become a self-fulfilling prophesy. Your family will benefit; we promise.

This is how the *building blocks* enter the picture, in the form of a simple algebraic equation:

Family Business Abundance = Engagement + Clarity + Scalability

We will spend most of our time together exploring the *Building Blocks* and discussing how to deploy them to your advantage.

MINDSET #2: Family Business Vs. Family-Owned Business

Most businesses in the United States are family-owned; yours probably is too. *Family Businesses* are a subset of *family-owned businesses*. This distinction is important, and whether you decide to embrace it or not, your perspective in this regard will have a significant impact on the future of your family.

In this book, a Family Business (intentionally capitalized) is defined as a family-owned business that purposefully involves multiple family members, always as thoughtful stakeholder owners, frequently as strategic contributors, and perhaps as active operators.

The concept of *ownership* may involve actual shares, legally held, or it may simply involve an emotional connection. The point is that *Family Business* can only flourish through intentional group effort, involving many, most, or all key family members. Ideally, this effort spans multiple generations, and it directly influences the way family members identify themselves and define their purpose.

Let's be clear: When it comes to Family Business, the business is a part *of* the family; it does not stand apart *from* the family.

MINDSET #3: The Family Business Growth Engine

In order to perpetuate long-term abundance, you need to continue to grow over time. Do not make the mistake of thinking that selling your business will provide for future generations. At best, that will lead to a scarcity mindset, and at worst, the money will run out much sooner than expected.

Liquidity events are not growth engines. A large bank balance may cover your immediate needs, and it may even take care of your children for a while after you are gone, but it will not last, because it will not be able to grow fast enough. The math is clear:

> Passive investment portfolios alone cannot sustain abundance across multiple generations.

If you still have an operating business, you are part way there, but you are not completely in the clear. You must keep *growing*. Without growth and transformation, your family enterprise is destined to peter out over time; entropy will inevitably set in, and competitors with new energy and technology will eat your lunch.

The challenge we face has two fundamental drivers. First, it is likely that your family will grow into the future as new children are born. And second, every year, each person will probably want to spend more than they did last year. That is human nature. It's all about family population and consumption. The surest way to overcome these dynamics is to build and grow operating companies that can outpace the expansion of your family's appetite for spending.

Of course, many families experience abundance without the help of a family business. However, this generally transpires one person at a time, or one branch at a time, through the cultivation of individual jobs and careers.

Investment portfolios augment individual achievement, and great investment advisors are worth their weight in gold. For families backed by strong careers and alternative forms of income, investment portfolios provide comfort and enrichment. More power to these families and their excellent advisors, but that's not what this book is about.

The *Growth Engine Mindset* asserts that sustainable abundance stems from concentrated, collective family effort. Your business provides the key.

BUILDING BLOCK #1: Engagement

Business owners tend to have a blind spot when it comes to integrating their families into their companies. Whether this is due to ignorance, laziness, distraction, or a combination of reasons, the outcome is generally the same. Business owners may provide summer jobs and various other benefits, but they often fail to engage their family members in an effective way. Most of their children never feel the spark of purpose and possibility that the family's business could provide. Owners may *think* they're involving their families, but judging from the results, many of them are fooling themselves.

How many families do you know who feel alienated from one other, or resentful of the businesses they own? How many young people never even consider entering the business? How many of these businesses unravel due to exhaustion, conflict, or lack of leadership? Do *you* ever worry about that?

When families engage properly, magic happens. The business becomes a member of the family, gaining strength from the family's collective thinking, energy, trust, and core values. It reflects and reinforces the purpose and core values of the family. That is why family businesses, even the publicly traded ones, tend to outperform their non-family peers. As a group, family businesses sustain better focus, they make more money, their quality is more consistent, and they endure for longer periods of time.

What makes the difference? How can you increase the likelihood that your family can thrive together? How can you avoid the isolation, disillusion, and dysfunctional conflict that families often experience?

Engagement is a major contributor, across all generations. It's crucial to start as early as you can, but it's rarely too late. Age-appropriate engagement can take root as early as the *Puppy Generation*, beginning at age four or five, and it can continue, with thoughtful and focused intensity, through the senior generation. You can make this happen.

The *Family Business Management System* incorporates six important elements of engagement. We call them *The Six Connectors*:

1. *Invitation*
2. *Purpose*
3. *Environment*
4. *Training*
5. *Trust*
6. *Resilience*

They will enable you to drive engagement into the *culture* and *behavior* of your family. We will discuss each of the Connectors in the chapters dedicated to Engagement.

BUILDING BLOCK #2: Clarity

Even families who are enthusiastically engaged can fail to succeed together if they operate in a fog. Lack of clarity is one of the most pernicious roadblocks that stands in the way of family business abundance.

So many people don't know how their business works, what they should expect, who has control of what, and what it takes to succeed. They don't see what they should *know* or what they should *do*. Often, they don't even understand why the business exists in the first place.

Does this sound familiar? Most families experience this, but you don't have to.

Trying to operate a business without clarity is like driving on a trip without a map, a speedometer, windshield wipers, or a gas gauge; maybe even without a destination in mind.

As with engagement, the management system emphasizes six key elements of transparency. We call them *The Six Clarities*:

1. *Vision*
2. *Transformation Plan*
3. *Priorities*
4. *Organization*
5. *Compensation*
6. *Control*

The clarities are concrete and practical, and if you implement the fundamentals, they will serve you well for a hundred years or more.

BUILDING BLOCK #3: Scalability

A well-tuned company will grow. Period. If you bake scalability into your business, then it will expand and thrive; it can't help it.

Here is the logic behind that assertion: If your business provides genuine value to the world, if your leadership and culture are effective and positive, if your business model can generate sustainable cash flow, if you have capable and well-aligned people, backed by solid infrastructure and productive work processes, your company will grow. This is what we call a *Natural Growth System*, and we help make it happen every day.

By working the *Family Business Management System*, you can double or triple the size of your enterprise, and that's just the beginning. It's simply a matter of time and focus, once you build true scalability into your organization. Spoiler alert: there are six *scalabilities* too:

1. *Leadership and Culture*
2. *Market Focus and Fit*
3. *Business Model and Finance*
4. *Team Alignment and Capacity*
5. *Infrastructure and Technology*
6. *Systems and Work Processes*

In the next chapter, we are going to meet two families. Their stories are similar, but the long-term outcomes they achieved are quite different. Every family is unique, of course, so comparisons like this aren't perfect, but it is helpful to scrutinize the two stories side-by-side, because they illustrate the key elements of our system.

Personal Note: *My Process*

I enjoy breaking things down, spreading them out, examining component parts, and reorganizing them to make better sense. Mom used to bring me her messed-up necklaces, and now my wife does too. I love untangling the knots until the chains lay clean and straight.

Business feels that way to me too. It is invigorating to distill messages to their core, reduce processes to essential steps. Reassembling the pieces in better order, revealing additional value, and crafting consistent, measurable, and repeatable ways to accelerate progress.

Of course, it's not just about breaking things down. There is also synthesis. Bringing the pieces together, drawing beautiful performance from discrete, individual parts. It's like music. I am a musician, a trumpet player and singer, and I love the way notes, discrete individual notes, come together with nuance and feeling to express a perfect phrase.

That's the way I regard a well-tuned business; discrete people, products, relationships, and processes, broken down to their essential components, then reassembled and delivered as a whole that is worth far more than the sum of its parts.

You can make it happen too. If you and your family dial into your business to that extent, you will be in position to scale the heck out of it. That's why we created the *Family Business Management System*.

FOOD FOR THOUGHT EXERCISE – YOUR PROCESS

Draw an image of your business in your mind. Think of it as a machine, a piece of music, a baseball game, or any other complex amalgamation. Choose your favorite metaphor, and then apply it to your business. Can you break it down in your imagination? Can you untangle the knots, perceive hidden connections, reassemble the pieces to add value?

Family relationships follow a similar pattern. Apply this thought experiment to your family for a quiet moment. Can you see the connections and relationships in a different light? Can you imagine that it's possible to resolve differences and frustrations, to leverage strengths and resources?

Now consider yourself. Are you new to the business or a veteran operator? In the game or on the sidelines? Whether you are joining your family business, staying with it, or transitioning from it, you are involved in a process too, a narrative with a beginning, a middle, and an end. Apply this component-level thinking to your career, your purpose, your future. Can you find patterns and opportunities that may not be apparent at first glance?

CHAPTER 3

Contrasting Stories: Two Car Guys

For many business-owning families, rather than enjoying ongoing growth and prosperity, members of the second and third generations watch their companies and their wealth slip away.

Here in the United States, people describe this phenomenon as *shirtsleeves to shirtsleeves in three generations*. In China, they say *rice paddy to rice paddy*. In Holland, it's *clogs to clogs*.

Here are two contrasting stories that prove this is not the inevitable result.

Car Guy Number One

In 1899, a boy was born on a hard-scrabble farm in Harvey, North Dakota. No electricity; no running water. The baby's parents, recent immigrants from Odessa in the Russian Empire, named him Herman, and for his middle name, they chose Harvey, after their new hometown. People called him HH for the rest of his life.

21

HH dropped out of school after the sixth grade so he could work on the farm, a sacrifice he would always regret. HH enjoyed farming, but the prospect of living on that small plot of land for the rest of his days haunted him from the beginning. Eventually, he became so restless that he needed to make a run for it. When he was still a teenager, HH hopped a freight train to Minnesota, where he became a mechanic and a salesman. Then, with new skills in tow, he worked his way down to South America, and he wound up selling and servicing agricultural equipment for the Minneapolis Moline Company.

After a few years in the plains of Brazil and Argentina, HH returned to North Dakota, to a city called Minot. And there, after his long journey, nearly back where he started, he found what he had been missing all along, a warm and humorous girl named Pauline McFarland. She was beautiful, she was educated, and according to most people, she was *big trouble*.

You see, Pauline's father was the president of the local college, and even *more* intimidating, prior to that, he had been the superintendent of schools for the entire Dakota Territories before statehood. Stern, proud, and serious, can you imagine *George McFarland, PhD* approving of a sixth-grade-educated, small-town farm boy, traveling salesman, and mechanic, for his youngest daughter's hand?

Pauline was *way* out of HH's league. She was intoxicating, but her family made HH feel provincial and small. Instead of giving up, however, he resolved that somehow, someday, he would change George McFarland's mind, earn his respect.

HH *burned* to be successful; he was hungry and determined. He became a voracious reader and a keen observer, while working extremely hard, day and night, pursuing his personal and financial goals.

HH went to work for an automobile distributorship as a mechanic and a salesman, and he excelled. Eventually, General Motors recognized his potential, and they granted him one of their first automobile *dealerships*, a franchise to sell Buicks and Cadillacs in Minot, North Dakota.

And more important, HH won George McFarland's approval. He and Pauline were married in the late 1920s, and in the early years, they had three children: James, Gerald, and Jill.

HH drove himself hard. He paid the price, sacrificed, learned, and grew. During the Great Depression, times were extremely tough, and while WWII was raging, there were few decent cars to sell because manufacturing was diverted to wartime production. Then, as always in North Dakota, there was the weather, a fickle and harsh adversary to the farmers and to the merchants who served them. Circumstances knocked HH down again and again, occasionally to the brink of disaster, but he got back up every time.

He eventually became a successful entrepreneur in mid-century North Dakota. Mind you, HH was no Rockefeller, but he prevailed. He earned widespread esteem, at home, at General Motors in Detroit, and perhaps most important, in the mind of McFarland. People admired HH as a businessman, an educated person, and a breeder of cattle and Tennessee Walking Horses.

HH was a co-founder of the local country club. He became an outdoorsman and active rancher, and as a member of the Vaqueros de Los Ranchos riding group, he and his favorite horse, *Gentleman Jim*, would board a train to California each year to join the annual spring roundup, where he rode for days with the likes of Walt Disney and Ronald Reagan.

By the end of his life at age eighty-eight, HH's car dealership had expanded to include Buick, Pontiac, Cadillac, Jeep, Honda, Volvo,

Subaru, Mercedes, and MG. This was quite an achievement, especially in a small market like Minot. At various points, HH also owned a window company, an appliance retailer, an electronics store, a boat dealership, a mental health clinic, a 6,000-acre cattle ranch, an alfalfa processing plant, and a substantial portfolio of commercial real estate properties. He also contributed generously to non-profit community organizations.

Please pause for a moment to consider the arc of this story. This is a tale of rags-to-riches success, do you agree? HH proved his worth. He made a fortune. He and Pauline had a wonderful family, and they traveled the world. They led exciting and fulfilling lives.

A happy ending? For HH and Pauline, certainly. For the rest of their family, *not so much.*

HH died a rich man, but his children experienced tremendous heartache. They were ill-equipped to run HH's remaining businesses interests, and they did not know how to be effective stewards of the wealth HH left behind. A few short years after his death in 1987, nearly everything was gone. *HH's family failed to sustain their growth engine for the long term.*

Today, all those companies, all that money, all that success, are a thing of the past. Rather than enjoying ongoing growth and prosperity, the second generation suffered through substance use disorders, multiple marriages, frustrated careers, and even suicide.

That is the fate of many family businesses, but it doesn't need to be.

This story had a major impact on my life, and in many ways, it has driven my career. HH Fisher was my grandfather.

Car Guy Number Two

Larry H. Miller was born in 1944. He grew up in a rather poor neighborhood in Salt Lake City, Utah. His house had electricity and indoor plumbing, at least, but that didn't make it the Ritz. It was good enough for Larry, however, a gateway to a neighborhood full of kids, fascinating natural wonders, and non-stop action.

Larry was a happy and curious kid. His birth father had left his mother when Larry was less than two years old, but that was okay. Larry's mother remarried a man whom Larry would love, respect, and refer to as Dad for the rest of his life.

Speaking of love and respect, when he was just fifteen years old, Larry fell for a wonderful young woman named Gail Saxton, and as with HH, her parents didn't want Larry around either. To be sure, the Saxtons weren't elitist academics, but they *did* call the shots, and they did *not* see much potential in this small, intense, seemingly undistinguished boy. (OMG, was *that* ever a monumental miscalculation.)

Larry was restless, energetic, and smart. He was driven by anxieties, aspirations, and an intensely competitive nature. He felt a visceral need to support his family and his community, and the fear of failing his family drove Larry relentlessly for many years. Like HH before him, he worked extremely hard to win and to succeed.

Larry had exactly twice as much formal education as HH; he made it through the twelfth grade. Extremely bright, Larry was a National Merit Scholar in high school, but he was too impatient for college. Larry stopped attending classes after only a few weeks at the University of Utah. Instead, he became his own teacher, and like HH before him, he was a lifetime learner. By the end of his life, Larry had received five honorary PhDs.

Larry's drive, intelligence, and competitive nature surfaced early on. Larry became the Utah State Marble Champion when he was only twelve years old, and shortly thereafter, he began pitching softball. Larry was a maniacal competitor, and he easily redirected his killer instinct from the marble circle to the softball diamond. Like Serena and Venus Williams, Michael Jordan, and Tiger Woods, Larry practiced for endless hours, every day, long before and after the other kids entered and left the field.

And the hard work paid off. Larry broke into the ranks of national fast-pitch when he was only sixteen years old, competing against hard-core adults, pitching and twice *winning* the softball equivalent of the World Series. In 1992, they inducted Larry into the Softball Hall of Fame in Findlay, Ohio.

Larry spent the early days of his business career playing semi-pro softball and working day jobs as a parts man in car dealerships. Applying his unique combination of wicked smarts and inhuman workloads, he consistently transformed parts-department operations, doubling, tripling, and more, the revenues and profits of these formerly moribund cost centers. Over time, Larry became a renowned parts-department *wizard*.

Larry and Gail finally acquired a dealership of their own, a Toyota store, in 1979, fifty-some years after HH got his.

Yes, that's right; Larry got the woman of his dreams too. He and his wife Gail had a strong marriage, and over time, they had five children, Roger, Greg, Bryan, Stephen, and Karen.

In addition to their business success, Larry and Gail passed remarkable kindness, generosity, and community awareness along to their children. By offering innumerable helping hands and contributions, large and small, public and private, the Miller family has become a much-loved, leading force for strengthening families, society, and culture, in Utah and beyond.

By the time he died in 2009, Larry and his family owned over forty auto dealerships and nearly fifty other businesses, including an innovative chain of movie theaters, a motorsports racetrack, a professional sports and concert arena, and an NBA basketball team. Approximately ninety companies in all, with combined annual revenues of over $3 billion at the time of his passing.

Several of Larry's family members were and are actively involved in the family business. In fact, Larry's family is *still* growing his group of companies. Some estimates peg the 2018 annual revenues of the Larry H. Miller Group of Companies between $5 and $6 billion.

A Tale Of Two Owners

HH Fisher and Larry H. Miller shared many characteristics, priorities, and behaviors in common. But the long-term outcomes for their families were substantially different.

HH Fisher's family was shirtsleeves to shirtsleeves. They had to start over after three generations. Larry H. Miller and his family built a multi-generational family empire that will likely endure for more than 100 years.

With so many similarities, why were the results so different?

That is one of the key questions driving this book. Why is it that some families succeed over the long-term, and some fizzle out after a generation or two? Is it *luck*, or is there something deeper and more intentional than that?

Many elements come into play, of course, but ultimately, families have more control than you might think. Mostly, it's about purpose, direction, and execution. You need a management system to succeed, and we have spent many years building one that fits the bill, a system that can enable you to build a story that works for you, *and* your family.

HH was a good man. He loved his family. He worked hard. He told the truth, and he lived up to his commitments. He contributed to his community, and he succeeded beyond the wildest dreams of a sixth-grade dropout from Harvey, North Dakota. But his mindset led him to neglect the three essential *Building Blocks* of Family Business Abundance: *Engagement, Clarity*, and *Scalability*.

HH failed to successfully *engage* his wife, children, and grandchildren in his business. They all worked in the company as kids, of course. Two of them even worked at the car dealership as adults. But in many ways, these were just jobs, not cultivated careers.

There was also a distinct lack of *clarity*. These were HH's companies, and he held his affairs close to his vest, mostly in his head. He could be temperamental and inconsistent, and no one ever knew exactly where they fit in along the way. When you don't know where you stand, it is hard to plan and commit, and the natural reaction is to retreat.

HH made the decisions, and he ran his companies with a tight fist, which, in the end, pushed away the people he needed most.

Finally, HH's enterprise was not *scalable*. His companies were separate, disconnected from one another. He ran them well, but he ran them *himself*, telling rather than teaching. He failed to cultivate a leadership team that could make decisions on their own, and he failed to develop a strategic vision or scalable infrastructure that could survive his passing.

And to top it off, HH became more careful and conservative as he aged. Rather than sustaining a growth mindset, he played it safe, selling off nearly all his businesses and real estate before he retired. By the time of his death, all that was left was the car dealership and a few buildings. His once thriving empire was largely reduced to a bank account, the *liquidity event* that so many entrepreneurs crave. In the end, this was not sustainable for his family.

Larry followed a different path. The early years of his journey were like HH's, characterized by single-minded focus, crippling workloads, and stubborn independence. The perspectives featured in this book took decades to crystalize in Larry's mind, but eventually they did, and that made a significant difference. A few years before he died, Larry realized that he didn't want to complete his journey by himself. He concluded that he wanted his business to extend beyond his individual existence. So, Larry intentionally cultivated a professional organization, and he purposefully *engaged* his family and trusted leadership colleagues.

In addition to engagement, Larry insisted upon *clarity*. This took courage, discipline, and constant communication. Larry's principles led him to make difficult decisions, and they forced him to withstand tremendous pressure along the way. For example, Larry nearly went broke building a new stadium for his beloved Utah Jazz basketball team, but he was convinced that he needed additional scale to counter difficult market trends, and he was determined that the team would never leave Utah. The team belonged to his family and his community, not just to him. Bottom line, everybody knew the mission and core values that drove The Larry H. Miller Companies, and whenever he could, he openly shared his priorities and plans with his family and senior managers.

Finally, rather than throttling back or selling off his assets, Larry continued to *scale* the heck out of his companies. He built a family *Growth Engine*, which enabled him to facilitate a solid transition to the next generation and beyond.

Personal Note: *Two Heroes*

HH Fisher was one of my first and most important heroes. Larry H. Miller is one of my heroes too. And although I'm sad to say I never got to meet Larry, I do know some of his family members. I have deep respect for them; the Millers are a family to be reckoned with.

I don't think HH and Larry ever actually met one another either, but who knows? Perhaps they did. I often wonder what their conversation would have been like. I imagine they would have enjoyed the exchange. They shared so many views and experiences in common.

By the way, please don't gather the wrong impression. My story through HH is not a personal tale of woe. Far from it. Every family face challenges. My siblings, my cousins, and I have had wonderful lives. We were privileged and happy as children. We went on to fulfilling careers and families of our own, and in my case, HH's experience provided a gateway to meaningful, rewarding work that provides joy and purpose every day.

We remain a close-knit family. We are fortunate, and each of us feels a profound sense of gratitude. However, our careers and assets are separate; we are each on our own. The businesses are gone, and we are not working together professionally. A once powerful economic engine has become silent and still.

This dynamic is common. I'll wager you can recall examples from your own community, family-owned businesses that withered or died before their time. Abundance may remain, but it is not long-term *Family Business Abundance*.

FOOD FOR THOUGHT EXERCISE – ENGAGEMENT, CLARITY, AND SCALABILITY

Those key building blocks make all the difference. Can you relate? Take a moment to consider how they apply to your personal situation and aspirations.

Later, we will think about your family, and your business. For now, just focus on yourself. Reflect for a moment upon the cases of HH Fisher and Larry H. Miller. Which one resembles your situation the most? With whom do you resonate?

How engaged are you in your family and in your family business today? If you're the founder or in the first generation, do you still have the spark and passion that led you to begin building in the first place? Are you pleased with your progress, afraid about what the future holds, or both?

If you're in the second, third, or later generation, where do the family and the business fit into your life? Are you actively leaning in? Do you feel a sense of belonging and ownership, or do you feel like an island, pursuing your own dreams, stepping to the beat of your own drummer?

How about clarity? Can you see where you stand? Are you clear about what the business is, how it works, who makes everything happen? Do you understand the relationships, metrics, and outcomes that drive the business and your family?

Are you ready to grow, as an individual and as a professional? Are you and your business on the path to scalability?

We will spend most of this book together exploring engagement, clarity, and scalability as they relate to your family and your business. But first, please take a moment to understand where the building blocks fit into your life before we get all revved up.

CHAPTER 4

Family Business Abundance

The first step on this journey is to acknowledge the rewards of family business abundance, and to decide for yourself that these rewards are worth the cost. Your journey will take courage, imagination, and sacrifice. Along the way, you will encounter uncertainty, risk, conflict, occasional boredom, financial distress, and chronic exhaustion. Without a potent conviction that the rewards outweigh the costs, you are likely to lose your way.

The three mindsets, especially this one, may seem obvious, perhaps even trivial, at first glance, but don't let that fool you. *It is obvious that successful business-owning families are rich*, that they have found material abundance, and it is tempting to stop at that surface level. But if you dive deeper, you will find sublayers of grit and insight that will help you endure for the long haul.

If it's not already there, you need to develop a vision in your mind's eye, an image of your success, an image accompanied by stubbornness, powerful and compelling enough to sustain you and your family through a long and difficult climb. The best way to begin developing this strength is to intentionally cultivate the mindset of this book, *Family Business Abundance.*

This mindset consists of two interlocking convictions. You must be able to honestly tell yourself:

> The rewards that come from family business success are greater than the sacrifice required to attain them. The climb is worth the view, by a wide margin, and I will dedicate my energy to getting there.
>
> We can do this. Many families have come before us, and we are every bit as worthy as they are. Our goal is attainable, and it is within our power to succeed together.

Those are some strong, intimidating words, so let's repeat the first core assertion of this book:

Over the long-term, family business is the most rewarding path you can take. If you approach it right, you and your family can thrive together across multiple generations.

If you intend to run this marathon, you must convince yourself that this is the best way to live your life, and that you can pull it off.

The *Family Business Abundance* mindset will comfort you and provide resilience as you trudge along the entrepreneurial path. It will sustain you through the conflict and fear. It will bring you peace by helping you know, deep down, that the answers will come, the obstacles will fall away, and that you and your family will create something with so much value and meaning that you would gladly do it all over again.

Adopting and sustaining this mindset requires a multi-step process. Let's get started:

Step One

Take a moment to consider the concept of *success*. How do you think it applies to families and companies in general, and to your family and business in particular? Close your eyes and imagine the *rewards* that could accompany that success. How does this make you feel? What do the notions of success and reward mean to you, deep down?

Visualize it: Fascinating challenges, millions of dollars, positive impact, status and respect, family togetherness. In your mind's eye, picture the house you will live in, the size of your bank account, your name on the front of a hospital or a library. Form a clear impression of the difference you want your business to have upon your life, your family, and the broader community.

Don't worry if you come up empty, afraid, or frustrated at first. Most people struggle with this. These questions are so big, it's hard to know where to begin addressing them. But we've been down this path before, many times. During our time together in this book, you will break the challenge down into bite-sized chunks.

Step Two

Consider what it could be like to work with your family under ideal conditions. Imagine collaborating with the people whom you love the most. Teaching one another, cultivating talents and relationships, building value, working together in harmony, pursuing worthwhile goals. Does this appeal to you? Some folks nod their heads yes; others run as fast as they can for the exit…

If you can get comfortable with this idea, take your thoughts to the next level.

Consider your family members, the people themselves, the generations that came before you, your own generation, and those who will follow. Some are still living, some yet unborn. Others have passed on but remain with us in so many ways. *What do you want for them?*

Seriously, think about your family for a moment. You probably don't do this consciously very often. Think hard. Run through the list. Dredge up the details that characterize every person.

When you think about your family, who comes into focus first? Is it your parents or grandparents? Are you picturing a spouse, perhaps children of your own? What about your siblings, nieces and nephews? Branching lines of aunts, uncles, and cousins. Do you have grandchildren to consider?

What about *you*, the you of your childhood, the you of today, and the person you have yet to become?

Gather them in your mind, invite them in, all together or one at a time. It doesn't matter. Run through the roster, conjure their faces. Allow the emotions in too. Relax, feel, and *pay attention.*

There is love there, I hope. Maybe some humor and affection, certainly pain, along with aspirations, on their behalf and for yourself. There must also be frustration and conflict, along with resentment, intimidation, and unanswered questions. All of these, of course! This is *family*; it's complicated, and sometimes it hurts.

Perhaps you'd enjoy working with some of these people. Others, not so much. Don't sweat the details; just open yourself up to the potential power of that collective group.

What is the value inherent in your people, the *Human Capital* that constitutes your family? What do those people know? What are their skills and talents? What are their capacities, individually and together? *How can you build upon what is already there?*

Step Three

Imagine an *excellent* organization, one that could endure for a hundred years or more. Solid and well-managed, with a clear mission, healthy culture, and inexorable growth. Now imagine that you and your family have built it. How would that feel?

Everyone has their place and knows where they are going. Your offerings are so valuable that people *line up* to buy! The trains run on time, and your business grows every year. What if financial worries were a thing of the past?

Your grandchildren and great-grandchildren continue to carry out your mission, bringing value to the world, in a concerted effort that was born before they were. Perhaps there are many companies, not just one.

Imagine what you and your family would do with the hundreds of millions, perhaps even *billions* of dollars your companies would give back to you over the coming decades. What experiences would you share? What changes would you bring forth in the world? How would you like to be remembered?

What? *Billions* of dollars?

Yes, you read it right. Hundreds of millions or even billions of dollars. The possibility is out there, for you and your family. The math is clear; we'll go through it in detail, two chapters from now.

This is not fiction; many multi-generational family businesses have made it happen. We have already discussed Larry Miller's family, and our culture provides many other examples, big and small. Here are just a few of the family businesses that have shaped the landscape of our country:

- The Ford Motor Company
- S. C. Johnson & Son, Inc.
- A. Schilling & Company
- Kendall-Jackson Vineyard Estate
- Doubleday Publishing
- Rand McNally
- Target Corporation (The Dayton Family)

- Corning Inc. (The Houghton Family)
- Fidelity (The Johnson Family)
- Hallmark Cards (The Hall Family)
- Andersen Corporation (Andersen Windows)
- Campbell Soup Company

And for every one of these gargantuan examples, there are thousands of small and mid-sized family businesses that deliver real value to their customers, their communities, and their families. It is a well-known fact that well-run family businesses provide more jobs, and generate higher profits, than non-family businesses, public or private.

But this not just about money, of course not, far from it. In fact, over the long term, money is arguably the *least* important outcome of family business. Successful families tell us, repeatedly, that in the end, the other rewards are far more precious than the financial ones.

A Broader Definition Of Abundance

Let us turn our thoughts to a broader definition of *abundance*, a more comprehensive view of family wealth.

It helps to think of wealth in terms of *family capital*. As mentioned above, there are multiple types of capital, extending far beyond tangible assets. People categorize family capital in multiple ways. The labels aren't that important. What matters is to acknowledge the scope of family capital, and to learn to distinguish between different types.

In the *Family Business Management System*, we refer to four categories of family wealth: financial capital, human capital, social capital, and enterprise capital.

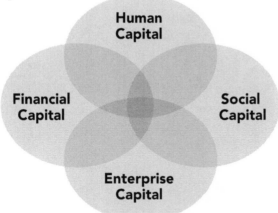

The word *capital* is key here, because it implies that like coins, bills, and precious gems, you can *accumulate* it. You can *store* it. You can *invest* it, *give* it away, and *spend* it. You can also squander it, if you're not careful.

Financial capital is easy. Well, perhaps not easy to acquire, but certainly easy to define. Financial capital includes anything that is tangible, inanimate, and carries a price tag, economic value that can be bought, sold, or bartered. Here are some examples:

1. Stocks, bonds, and currency

2. Companies, patents, and trade secrets

3. Private fund investments, public fund holdings, and real estate properties

4. Personal property, including homes, vehicles, lawn mowers, clothes, toys, and power tools

Simple economics; that is how people generally measure the wealth of a family. *"They're worth a million dollars."* Or twenty million, one hundred million, or a billion.

Tip of the iceberg is such a time-worn phrase, but the iceberg metaphor persists because there is much truth behind it, and it certainly applies here. Over the long term, Family Business Abundance is *far* more than money. It is *mostly* about people, relationships, and accomplishments.

Human capital refers to the people *inside* the family. This may seem less tangible than money, but often you *can* quantify it, and you can always appreciate it. Here are some examples, not an exhaustive list:

1. Relationship bonds, protection, and common interest

2. Affection, friendship, and love

3. Goodwill, kindness, and support

4. Intellectual capacity, education, curiosity, and intuition

5. Knowledge, skills, and judgement

6. Creativity, energy, and leadership

7. Spiritual power, understanding, and commitment

8. Perseverance, resilience, and grit

9. Physical strength, earning potential, and influence

Who are the people in your family? What are they good at, and where do they come up short? Individually and as a group, what do your family members bring to the table, and to the world? How much power do they have, and what could they accomplish, given enough time?

That is your human capital. Hold it close, and never underestimate or squander its value.

Social capital looks *outside* the family. This encompasses the advantages and options that stem from accomplishments and contributions to the community. Here are some examples:

1. Reputation, goodwill, and trust

2. Friendships, alliances, and partnerships

3. Loyalty from customers, suppliers, and employees

4. Political influence, sources of information, and benefit of the doubt

5. Freedom to maneuver, *deal flow*, and options

6. Community value, gifts, and impact

How do you put a price tag on that? Maybe you can't, but there is a ton of value there. Also, social capital endeavors, such as philanthropy and collective volunteering, provide a powerful gateway to family engagement and purpose. This is an important tool you can employ to attract and retain the attention of upcoming generations.

Enterprise capital represents a hybrid of the other three types. You may find it redundant, but we believe it is worth considering on its own. In her excellent 2015 book *Engaged Ownership: A Guide for Owners of Family Businesses* our friend Amelia Renkert-Thomas defines enterprise capital as follows:

> *"Enterprise capital is all the unique knowhow embodied within the business and the family; it is the array of one-of-a-kind combinations of capital that generate a return greater than the separate elements would generate individually. Enterprise capital is the end result of human capital that has been coupled with financial capital to accomplish a specific endeavor."*

Here are some examples of enterprise capital:

1. Mission, core values, and long-term strategic vision

2. Patents, trade secrets, and workflow process

3. Industry knowledge, commercial intuition, and seasoned judgement

4. Commercial connections, contracts, and joint ventures

Each of these was either mentioned above or can occupy a position in one or more of the other categories. It's the blend of business, human, and social rewards that sets this category apart.

A Personal Note: *A Debt of Gratitude And The Gift of Purpose*

Back in 2002, our friend Jay Hughes first made me aware that there were multiple forms of family capital. After that, I refined my understanding through conversations with Fredda Herz Brown, Fran Lotery, and Dennis Jaffe. Then, more recently, with Amelia Renkert-Thomas, who introduced the concept of enterprise capital. As far as I know, she invented that term, and I'm glad she did, because it is truly helpful. We appreciate each of those friends and collaborators.

I am so grateful for the help I've received, which leads me to highlight the power of gratitude itself, the first cousin to abundance. Gratitude, coupled with purpose, is the best way, perhaps the *only* way, to instill consistent feelings of contentment, fulfillment, and occasionally even happiness, into your life and the culture of your family.

Please let me know if you're curious about the power of gratitude and purpose. We could have a long conversation about those priceless gifts. They drive us forward and provide the foundation for the work we do. At Featherstone, we have acquired and developed several techniques and activities that can help you cultivate both within your family. Check out our web site for specific resources.

FOOD FOR THOUGHT EXERCISE – YOUR FAMILY CAPITAL INVENTORY

I encourage you to think about the capital your family possesses today. If you were to draw up a Family Capital Balance Sheet, what do you think the main categories would be?

How would you quantify your family's financial resources? Not an easy task, is it? Especially if you have multiple generations and households to wrestle with. It's worth the effort, though. At the very least, simply consider the question at a high level. Make a rough estimate.

Now, think about the human side. Consider yourself and your family members. Who are you guys? What do you know, and what are you capable of achieving? Make a list of your human capital, in your mind or on paper. If the human dimension of your family was a bank account, what would the balance be?

What social impact does your family have? What good things do you and your family members bring to the world, individually and collectively? And what does your family receive from the world in return?

Finally, think about the link between your family and your business. Regarding your enterprise capital, what does your family know, and what capacities does it enjoy as a direct result of its experience with the company?

Family Business Vs. Family-Owned Business

Consider for a moment your family pet. *Whose dog is it, really?* Likewise, when you think about the relationship between your family and your business, who does it *belong to*, really?

Is your business the domain of one person, a lone entrepreneur, or does the enterprise belong to all of you, young and old together? Is this truly a Family Business, or is it someone's individual sandbox?

Whether you're aware of it or not, this distinction has had, and will continue to have, a huge impact on your family's fortunes.

Now consider this: Do you have a Family Business? Do you want one?

The answers to these questions may seem obvious but think again. You or someone in your family may *own* a business, but does that make it a Family Business?

We define a Family Business (with the F and B capitalized) as community property, not just the domain of one or two individuals. Philosophically speaking, the family *owns* the business together, across multiple generations.

Please consider three questions about your company:

1. How would you describe the relationship between your business and your family?

2. Does your business feel like a member of the family or separate from it?

3. Who *owns* your company?

That last query calls for an explanation. For a moment, ignore the technicalities of who holds individual shares.

Is Yours A True Family Business?

If you have a true Family Business, multiple family members feel a sense of active ownership and engagement, even if they don't work there. The company anchors the family's legacy, and in turn, family members feel responsible for upholding the company's mission and core values.

That's not the way most business owners play the game. Most owners try to *separate* their families from their business. They believe that putting emotional distance between those two sides of their lives will help them cope, keep things in perspective. Can't you just hear them thinking:

"Compartmentalization. That's an important skill, right? Something to be proud of, a sign of strength. James Bond does it, so do heart surgeons, astronauts, and big-time CEOs. Focus on the task at hand. Results are what counts. Get the job done. This is *my business*. Business is business. Family is family. Keep them separate; nothing personal. If my business does well, our family will be fine."

Hogwash, I say.

People who think this way are fooling themselves. Your family is no more separate from your business than you are from the air you breathe.

Why is this important? Because, if you try to keep your family and your business apart or let the relationships drift on their own, then you are ignoring reality, you are missing a great opportunity, and you are planting the seeds for future suffering.

We already discussed a pair of contrasting examples. HH Fisher and Larry H. Miller were separated by geography and time, but they were united by a common love of entrepreneurship, family, and the automobile.

HH had a successful entrepreneurial career. He died a wealthy man, after a long and happy marriage that produced three children and seven grandchildren. For the most part, HH's family was close and loving, and it remains mostly united to this day. However, there was tremendous heartache in the second generation, all the businesses are gone, and the wealth became dissipated within a few short years. HH's family business abundance is now history.

HH loved his children and grandchildren without question, but this was *his* adventure, framed within the arc of *his* lifetime. His enterprise may have been family-owned, but it was not a Family Business, not in the way we defined it above. Among other factors, this perspective led to eventual dissolution.

Bottom line: *HH Fisher was a lone-wolf entrepreneur.* He considered the businesses to be *his,* separate from his family. HH was the entrepreneur; he was the *owner.* This was a family-*owned* business, but he never made it a Family Business, not really.

Larry Miller's story stands in contrast to HH's. By the way, Larry nearly missed this boat too; he started out every bit as focused and control oriented as HH, but he managed to catch himself. Over time, Larry concluded that his group of companies extended beyond his personal control. He declared that his purpose was to create a Family Business, and in some respects, even perhaps even a *community* business. This perspective drove Larry to cultivate the building blocks that lead to multi-generational success.

When he died, Larry left behind a powerful growth engine, along with a family and an organization that was structured, fully engaged, and capable of expanding the empire into the future.

What Do You Want For *Your* Family?

Which perspective rings true for *your* family today? Which perspective do you *want*?

Most business owners follow the *lone-wolf* path. We call it *The Entrepreneur's Journey.* This perspective comes naturally, because popular culture has been packing that myth into our heads for thousands of years.

What! Thousands of years? What does that even *mean*?

Back in the last century, a philosopher and historian named Joseph Campbell researched and popularized a concept he called The Hero's Journey. He became quite popular for a while, and he wrote about this in multiple books, including his 1949 classic *The Hero With A Thousand Faces.*

In his writings, Campbell noted that thousands of years before humans learned to write, they began transmitting knowledge through storytelling, and we continue that practice to this day.

Well, you might say, *that's* obvious. Of course, cavemen used stories. What else did they have to do, sitting there by the fire after a hard day of clubbing one another and escaping from saber-toothed tigers? Everybody tells stories. We're using them here in the book because they stick in people's minds. They provide useful shortcuts that drive home conclusions and leave lasting imprints. What's the big deal?

Well, on the surface, it *is* obvious, but Campbell took this concept a step further. Not only have all cultures told stories, he contends, they basically tell the *same* stories, over and over and over and over and over again. The Hero's Journey archetype is particularly relevant to our discussion.

Every culture, living and extinct, has fostered myths and legends of *lone heroes*, individual men and women who accomplish extraordinary things against great odds. We constantly celebrate these stories, and they nearly always follow a similar pattern.

A young man or woman comes into the story amid comfortable surroundings. Think of Belle in *The Beauty and the Beast*, Bilbo Baggins in *The Hobbit,* or Gilgamesh, the ancient Sumerian king. Innocently minding his or her own business, our soon-to-be hero's peaceful existence becomes threatened or shattered when he or she encounters an enticing opportunity, or an alarming crisis compels them to leave their comfortable home in search of resolution or reward.

Once our heroes leave their villages, they generally go through a phase of isolation, spending extended periods "in the wilderness." Then after a time, often with training and counsel from a sage— they venture out to slay dragons, snatch the magic ring, or obtain blueprints for the Death Star, saving damsels, vanquishing evildoers, and acquiring great rewards along the way.

Sadly, some of these men and women make the ultimate sacrifice, but those who survive return home to a hero's welcome, where they live happily ever after, blessed by their victories. Does that sound familiar? Consider the stories of Odysseus, George Washington, Jesus Christ, Harry Potter, and Luke Skywalker. They are all variations of the same archetypal narrative, told repeatedly.

Here's the punchline: *The Hero's Journey* rhymes with the way we characterize entrepreneurs.

Entrepreneurs are the heroes of today; they are *our* version of Hercules.

Now, take that a step further: Entrepreneurs usually view *themselves* as heroes. Lone wolves. And even more important, their *families* buy into the myth as well, so they ignore the company, or at least fail to bake it into their personal plans.

Here's a typical scenario.

Our entrepreneurial hero leaves her comfortable job, perhaps because she was fired, or she recognized a wonderful business opportunity. She spends months or years in the wilderness, struggling to find a solution, invent a new technology, acquire the money she needs, and is often aided by a mentor, coach, or wise investor along the way.

Eventually, after enduring tremendous stress, solving gnarly problems, testing new formulas, and avoiding financial catastrophe, she emerges victorious, returns home a hero, buys a mansion, and lives happily ever after. Sound familiar? I have played that role myself, multiple times. Perhaps you have too.

It is a *fine* story, dramatic and inspiring. However, by sticking to this perspective, lone-wolf entrepreneurs separate their businesses from their families, and they miss the boat. They constrain their companies to their individual lifespans and capabilities.

HH was a lone-wolf entrepreneur, a dragon-slayer. His rendition of *The Hero's Journey* separated HH's family from his companies. And his family members followed suit; they bought into the lone-wolf perspective as well. They thought: "This is HH's business; father built this company." Through this lens, they failed to realize that they could *participate*, that they could devote *their* lives too, that they had the opportunity to build an enduring enterprise *together*.

We're not naive. This won't be easy, and it might take a while, particularly if you need to overcome trust issues or years of family-business separation. But if you open yourself to the possibility and then start pushing, you will be amazed by the transformation that takes place.

Where To Start

Start by asserting that this is a shared challenge, a family journey, not just your business, not the property of a lone entrepreneur.

Make your company a Family Business, not just a family-owned business. Make it work for your whole family.

When we discuss the concept of family business with our clients, we find it useful to propose a one-hundred year timeframe. This rewires our point of view from the *entrepreneur's journey* to the *family's journey*.

An essential step along the way to *Family Business Abundance* involves publicly acknowledging that the family is in this together, for the long term. The business is a member of the family, with its own agenda, baggage, and potential for conflict, just like any other.

Based on all this, I'll ask you again: Is your business a *Family Business*?

A Personal Note: *I Wanted To Be A Hero*

I started my career as a lone-wolf entrepreneur, like my grandfather, HH. In fact, I consciously wanted to be *just like him*, and I was hard core. I emulated HH Fisher with intensity. I started and ran several businesses. Along the way, I raised several million dollars in venture capital, learned how to sell, how to build a team, and how to draw value from a functional board of directors.

It never even occurred to me to share my company with my family, that my wife and I could become gen-one members of a *Family Business* of our own.

The companies were *mine*; this was *my* career. I worked myself to the bone, ignoring the stress, compartmentalizing my focus, separating my businesses from my family, and keeping a stiff upper lip. Just like HH before me. In many respects, those were anxious and lonely years, and after a great deal of solo struggle, I finally saw that I was failing with that approach.

Over time, I found a metaphor that helped me cope with the pressures and anxieties. This idea helped me communicate the strong feelings I had for the company I was building, and it helped me mitigate the sacrifices of time, money, and attention that business-building forced me to make.

I began to consider my company to be another one of our children. I began telling myself, my wife, and other people that we had *three* kids: our two sons, Tucker and Brooks, and our business. That metaphor, *company as family member,* conveyed a powerful and comforting perspective for me back then. It helped me open the business up to them, and to reduce my isolation and stress, just a bit.

Looking back, I can see that my early version of the metaphor was incomplete, but it helped me, and it represented the first step in understanding the concept of *Family Business Abundance,* with broader implications than I realized at the time.

FOOD FOR THOUGHT EXERCISE – YOUR FOUNDER STORY

Ruminate about or write down the story of your company. How did it start? Who were the initial players? What dreams did they hold together, and what obstacles did they overcome?

Where is the business today, and how does it relate to your family?

What are the aspirations for your business into the future? What could it look like twenty, fifty, or a hundred years from now?

Tell the story from your perspective. See what comes up, organize your memories, and feel the emotions.

If you feel stuck, try exploring the story from two points of view, the entrepreneur's journey, and the family's journey. What feels more authentic looking back, and which do you prefer going forward?

Share your story with your family. Ask them what they think; spark the conversation. You could challenge people to compose their own narratives. If you do, where is the common ground? What aspects of the story are under dispute?

If the story is clear in your mind, and if you can extend that clarity to others, it will encourage and help sustain you, strengthening your sense of purpose and direction. This is one of many important gifts you can give yourself and your family.

Chapter 6

Family Business Growth Engine

Oprah Winfrey once said: "Be thankful for what you have; you'll end up having more. If you concentrate on what you don't have, you will never, ever have enough."

We have met, collaborated with, and advised hundreds of families over the years, many of whom you would recognize from their products, logos, and TV commercials. Based upon those relationships, we can confirm the well-worn truism that money doesn't make you happy.

Money may not make you happy, but that doesn't mean you shouldn't go for it.

Money is an *amplifier*, a multiplier of happiness, but also of sadness and strife. Money makes the good things better, and the bad things worse. It can set you free, or it can condemn you and your family to misery.

But before we get all mushy about this, let's get practical and dive into some numbers. Let's pretend for a moment that money is the point, the most important thing. That leads us now to spin one of our fundamental assertions:

> Over the long term, a Family Business is arguably the most lucrative strategy a family can take.

Another Tale Of Two Families

Consider the stories of two families, the Davis family and the Michaels family. Similar beginnings; different endings.

Ronald Davis was a contractor, a builder of homes and small office buildings. Constance Michaels was a retail pioneer, the founder of a shoe store that grew across multiple communities, eventually morphing into a diversified retail conglomerate that spread across the western United States.

Although their industries could hardly have been more different, Connie and Ron followed remarkably similar paths. They both started their businesses when they were single. They each got married and had children during the early days of growth, and they both struggled mightily to build their companies, learning the hard way, taking risks, suffering setbacks, and ultimately achieving success. One stayed married. The other did not.

Davis Construction and Connie's Closet both launched in the same year, 1949. After typical rough start-up periods, the companies grew for twenty years. By the end of 1969, each company had achieved annual revenues of $20 million, with cash flow of $4 million and net income of $2 million. Identical financial performance.

Quick Note: Unlike the other stories in this book, these examples are *entirely* made up. We did this on purpose to make the math easy.

Profitability ratios, sales price, valuations, growth and spending are identical and over-simplified in order to help us compare apples to apples. We even ignored taxes. Please don't get hung up on the details. The margins, take-out multiples, spending, and other factors are realistic and achievable. It's big-picture, directionality math that counts here.

Ron decided to sell his construction company in 1969, after concluding that it was time to kick back and enjoy the good life. Connie kept her business. She changed the name to Constance Collective. Her family, already deeply involved in the operation back then, continues to build it to this day.

By the way, to put things in perspective, in that same year, 1969, the United States put men on the moon and brought them safely back to Earth, the Beatles gave their last public performance, Boeing 747s took their first flights, and the Stonewall riots erupted in New York City. *What a moment in time.*

Let's see how the decision to sell or continue building played out for each family as of today, fifty years later. As mentioned above, we will stick to identical math whenever we can in order to keep the comparisons as close as possible.

Ron got a solid deal for his company. He sold it for six times cash flow, which means 6x $4 million, for gross proceeds of $24 million. After broker and legal fees of 8 percent, this left Ron and his family with a bit over $22 million. *Not bad at all.*

Ron was a prudent man, so he found a solid investment advisor who built a portfolio for the Davis family that delivered consistent annual growth of 7 percent. That's respectable for a balanced portfolio, especially considering the ups and downs of the economy that stretched from 1970 until today.

In another sign of prudence, Ron carefully restricted his family's spending to 5 percent of the portfolio each year, an amount that his advisors recommended in order to sustain the portfolio across multiple decades. That meant $1.1 million of spending in 1970, *not too shabby*, and it grew from there as the portfolio gained value over time.

After all that growth and all that spending, Ron Davis and his family ended up with $60 million dollars in 2019, fifty years later. Sixty million dollars, and a very nice life. That is a story of family business success, no doubt about it.

But what happened to Connie? Remember, she decided to keep her company, and as coincidence has it, her company grew at the exact same rate as Ron's investment portfolio, 7 percent per year. And here's another coincidence, Connie's family spent the exact same amount as Ron's family, every year, to the penny (how *convenient* for the story*)*.

Okay, so after a nice liquidity event and fifty years of portfolio growth, with prudent spending, Ron ended up with $60 million dollars in the bank. You certainly can't argue with that outcome.

But wait. Guess what Connie's estate is worth at the end of 2019, including the re-invested proceeds from annual net income. Remember, she had exact same growth rate and exact same spending. Give it a good guess before you sneak a peek. The answer is on the following page:

$1.3 billion

Now *there's* an argument for multi-generational family business.

Family Economics

Time to come back down to Earth. When it comes to family financial capital, the fundamental equation is simple:

Financial Capital = (Initial Assets + Investment Returns + New Income) – (Consumption + Taxes)

Bigger is better, for the most part. We want the largest pile of initial assets, and we want the highest-possible investment returns. And the more additional income we can throw into the mix, the better.

On the other hand, we do not want more consumption, and we want to minimize taxes (Legally and ethically, of course). In a perfect world, that number would go *down* over time, but of course, it rarely does.

Consumption drains the pile. It usually starts as a nonissue. Wealth generators typically don't spend that much, and besides, there aren't that many people at the trough at first; nuclear families tend to be small.

However, over time, the consumption monster often grows and grows and *grows*. This equation is simple too, but now, as you can see, the natural dynamics are working against us:

Consumption = (Number of family members) x (Average spending per family member)

The dynamics hurt us in two ways. First, the population of the family increases over time, and second, each of the individual family members wants to spend more money this year than they did last year. This is a recipe for long-term scarcity, and it's inevitable, unless you have an engine that can pump substantial amounts of new income into the system.

It is nearly impossible to generate enough long-term family capital from passive investment portfolios. The math just simply doesn't work, unless you pack your portfolios full of unreasonably risky assets.

The primary objective of most investment portfolios is to preserve initial buying power, to support a family's current spending rates and perhaps provide some inheritance to a fortunate few as time goes by. Across multiple generations, most passive portfolios simply cannot keep up.

Consider the family population as generations multiply across time:

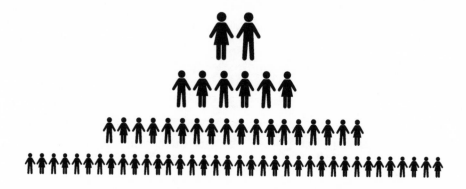

Skeptical readers might conclude that this graphic seems too aggressive. In fact, one of our early readers *did* raise that objection. "So many children per generation. Surely that's exaggerated to make the point, right?"

Well, he had us there, so we dug into the numbers, and what we found was interesting.

The rate of children-per-couple for zero population growth is approximately 2.1. That means that if every woman in the world had 2.1 kids, we would simply replace ourselves and the global population would remain constant. I'm happy to report that most of the developed world, including China, is trending in that direction. For example, according to World Bank statistics, in 2016, the number of births per woman in the United States was 1.8. In China, it was 1.62, and in Japan, the number was 1.44. According to Statistica, in 2018, births-per-woman in the U.S. had increased slightly to 1.9.

But hang on a minute. Just because we have zero population growth in general, it doesn't mean that our families don't *grow*. If families stay together, they still expand over time relative to the fortunes of the first generation. To illustrate this point, the following table shows family population growth across the years and generations.

Children per Family	Year 1	Years 25	Year 30	Year 75	Year 100
	G1 + G2	+ G3	+ G4	+ G5	+ G6
1.8	3.80	8.84	17.91	34.24	61.63
1.9	3.90	9.41	19.88	39.77	75.56
2.0	4.00	10.00	22.00	46.00	92.00
3.0	5.00	17.00	53.00	161.00	483.00
4.0	6.00	26.00	106.00	426.00	1,704.00

As before, our assumptions are purposefully simple, perhaps *too* simple; but again, it's directionality that counts. The chart assumes that each generation extends for 25 years, that the first-generation couple (G1) has had all their children by the time they start their business, and that all children are born when the prior generation is 25-years old. It also assumes that every child gets married, and that each person lives between 75 and 100 years.

Before you object to the oversimplification, consider the fact that the chart does *not* include multiple spouses, the children that result from those additional marriages, or the fact that some couples will have more children than average.

By the way, please note the difference between 1.8 and 4.0 children-per-generation. I am always amazed by the power of exponential growth. If every couple has 1.8 children per generation, the family will end up with 62 members in 100 years. But if every couple has 4 children per generation, the family will have 1,704 members in 100 years! An astounding difference, but that's how compounding works.

Now, let's move on from population to consumption per person.

Consumption tends to grow proportionally faster than the population of the family, because people get used to being rich and each person generally spends more over time. This is a natural human tendency. We gradually begin to feel entitled. We take it for granted that we deserve to live in upscale homes, to drive nice cars, to fly first class, and to wear beautiful things.

Regardless of the math, the bottom line is clear: *Without a Family Business Growth Engine, it always comes down to a race against time.*

Sometimes consciously, often unconsciously, smart people ask themselves: "How long can our investment portfolios outpace the exponential growth of our population and our spending?"

That's one of the reasons why people get depressed after they sell their businesses. Deep down, whether they realize it or not, they understand that their wealth has already started disappearing.

Let's go back to the math. Consider the $22 million liquidity event Ron enjoyed for the sale of his company. At 5 percent spending, Ron, his spouse, and their three children could each spend an average of $220,000 per year. Not bad in 1969. And today? At $60 million, they would share $3 million, which means $600,000 each. The problem is, by the time today rolled around, there are no longer only five family members. There are now *twenty, perhaps even forty*. That means every person receives from $75,000 to $150,000 each year. Still pretty good, but it's hard to live in mansions and fly first-class on that. And by the way, this assumes that the family was able to discipline itself to a 5 percent spending rate. Chances are, they could not have held that line, and the money would have run out long ago.

Shirtsleeves to shirtsleeves. Not a happy picture. *Believe me, I've been there.*

This dynamic naturally leads families to embrace the concept of stewardship. What a *nice* word, especially on the surface. Too bad that it often masks the incipient long-term problem we just discussed. Wealthy families *love* to talk about stewardship. It makes them feel like they are doing something about the problem, stemming the tide of entropy. Sometimes they're right, but most often, they're not.

Don't get me wrong. Stewardship is a *crucial* concept, a wonderful notion, especially among financial families who have sold their businesses and wish to fund their economic lives with passive investment portfolios.

Stewardship is a *good* and healthy philosophy regarding wealth. It is strategic and noble, but if a family does not have an engine to generate new wealth, their commitment to stewardship will lead to pervasive feelings of scarcity, sometimes even helplessness, no matter how rich they are.

Your Daily Choice

Please don't misinterpret the message. As we've mentioned before, we are *not* saying you shouldn't sell your business. In fact, we believe that you should always operate any business as if you intend to sell it, and you should always be prepared to do so, every day. But you should also operate the company for the *future*. Every day, business owners have three essential choices. They can sell the business, accept the status quo, or try to drive transformation.

Here's a picture:

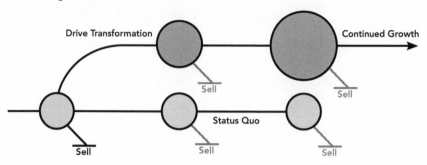

If you do, or already did, decide to sell your business, the question is: What does your family do after the sale? Do you rely upon passive investments, or do you reinvest in new businesses, in fresh entrepreneurial efforts?

We will discuss this concept further in the following chapters dedicated to engagement. For now, we'll simply assert that families who have healthy operating companies, families who bring tangible value to customers every day, who have the capacity to actually *expand* their family capital—human, social, enterprise, and financial—tend to have a more positive outlook on life.

Simply stated:

> Entrepreneurial families are more likely to experience the world in terms of abundance.

Bottom line: If your family has a Growth Engine, life often looks like a sunny day. If you don't, threatening clouds are always on the horizon.

A Personal Note: *Abundance Vs. Scarcity*

I have worked with so many individuals and families over the years. Each is unique, of course, and I love them all (well, at least *most* of them).

One characteristic I always pay attention to is their relationship to their money. That tells a lot about a family. Perhaps I'm extra dialed into this because I've had ups and downs of my own, but I am fascinated by the different ways people view the world in terms of abundance and scarcity.

I have personally known families with hundreds of millions of dollars in the bank who feel broke, and I know upside-down entrepreneurs who feel infinitely rich.

Of course, individuals within families tend to share similar abundance/scarcity mindsets, but not always. There is variation among family members, of course, sometimes significant variation, but family culture is *so* strong.

It's also important to recognize that individual people and nuclear family units can achieve abundance through jobs and other sources of personal income. You certainly don't have to be an entrepreneur or business owner to feel a nice sense of abundance in life.

However, one of the things I love the most about working with business owners is the impact that strengthening their business can make on a family's outlook on abundance. This isn't the only factor, of course, but I am convinced that the capacity to create new family capital is at or near the top of the list of things that generate a culture of contentment, satisfaction, and even happiness.

That's why I push so hard for families to build and maintain an entrepreneurial growth engine that can sustain their abundance across multiple generations. Go ahead, sell your business, but be sure to start another one that can take its place.

FOOD FOR THOUGHT EXERCISE – COUNT YOUR BLESSINGS

That's a well-worn aphorism, a cliché we've been tossing at ourselves and our kids without much thought. Well, it's time to open your eyes and consciously take stock.

Grab your trusty imagination or notebook and start drafting a gratitude list. Organize it however you want. I like putting things into categories: family, health, knowledge, possessions, etc. It doesn't matter, especially at first.

Stream of consciousness. That's how you get started with this exercise…

What are you grateful for? What are you happy you have, and what are you glad you don't?

I bet you can toss out fifty things… a pretty profile, a nice view, a sunny day, a warm sweater, a bit of arcane knowledge, the love of a friend, the absence of guilt. I bet you could toss out a million things if you really tried.

You will be amazed at the power of gratitude. If you consciously build gratitude into your life, I guarantee it will make you happier. It will change your life by cultivating feelings of abundance.

Give it a few minutes, right now. Purposely consider the things you're grateful for and be sure to include things that you are grateful to have avoided.

Now review your list with your family and your business in mind. How many positive experiences, things, and relationships have resulted from them? What family business abundance do you have in your life? How much more do you want?

Chapter 7

Family Business Abundance Manifesto

Family Business is hard, but despite the challenges, we are dedicating our volition and careers to the notion that our family can thrive and succeed together across multiple generations, for one-hundred years or more.

We consciously assert the following:

#1. Family business abundance is an excellent goal, well worth striving for.

"We believe that Family Business is the best way to accumulate wealth across multiple generations, including human, social, enterprise, and financial capital. Our family is fully capable of achieving multi-generational success, and we dedicate ourselves to making it happen."

#2. Our enterprise will be a Family Business, not just a family-owned business.

"Our business is part of our family, not separate from it. Even if we don't own shares today, each of us, young and old, is directly connected to our business, and we all feel a sense of ownership. We influence the company with our attitudes and actions, and in turn, we intentionally allow our business to influence us."

#3. A Family Business Growth Engine will sustain our family for the next 100 years or more.

"We will be more likely to view the world through a lens of abundance, thanks to our ability to generate substantial new capital for our family, which will enable us to overcome the feelings of scarcity that stem from family population growth and increased individual consumption."

Family Business is not just an idea or a category, it is a *way of life*. We consciously accept this and define ourselves in these terms. That is how multi-generational magic happens.

When we embrace our manifesto and harness the three mindsets, we begin to see our family and our company in a new light. We strive to leverage this awareness to our advantage, to up our game, to smooth out rough edges, to enhance our relationships, and to strengthen our business.

CHAPTER 8

The Principles Of Engagement

Firs things first. If we're going to talk about engagement, we must start with *you*. We need to determine where *you* stand in all of this.

Put Your Own Oxygen Mask On First

How many times have we listened to, or tried to ignore, flight attendants giving us that advice? It's a well-worn phrase, but once again, it survives for a reason. Remember, first and foremost, this book is about *you*.

You need to be firmly in the game before you start worrying about your family.

Think back to your founder's story. Where do *you* fit in? Are you the founder, the matriarch or patriarch? Maybe the founders were your parents, or grandparents, like mine were. Perhaps you're way down on the line, five, six, even seven generations removed from the big bang.

Who *are* you, anyway? How are *you* engaged?

Now, stop for a moment and consider this question with focused intention:

> How do your family and your business fit into your life?

What impact do you want to have upon the business, and what impact do you want the company to have upon you? Think hard. It could take decades for this to play out, so you don't have to have the answer today, but you had better put some calories into it.

Do you want to work for the company? Fulltime? Dedicate your career to it? Do you want to actively help fulfill its mission, promote its core values? Do you want to *lead* the company, now or someday in the future?

Maybe you have other ambitions. That's okay. Perhaps you simply want to help *sustain* the business, participate from a distance. Would you prefer to serve in a board capacity, or inject your opinion from time to time as a well-informed owner?

Do you dream of selling the business, redeploying the assets in directions that resonate more closely with your heartbeat?

Your future is coming, whether you like or not. Please don't kick this can down the road.

After you've bent your brain thinking about how *you* fit in, take some time to clear your head. Maybe take a quick walk, eat some comfort food, watch a sitcom, or listen to a piece of music.

Your Family Comes Next

Feel better? *Good.*

Now, it's time for an even bigger job. Set yourself loose on your family members. Focus your mind on them with conscious attention.

Are you a parent? If not, do you intend to be? If so, what role do you want your business to play in the lives of your children? If you have one, where does your spouse or significant other fit in? What about your siblings?

Which of your family members are going to lead this company, now and into the future? What do you want, from and for each of them? *Think* about it.

Then there's the upcoming generations, grandchildren, nieces, nephews...cousins, those great destroyers of family wealth. How will they relate to the business and to one another?

You ignore these questions at your peril.

A Difficult Challenge Ahead

Each family is so different; it's best not to generalize. However, most families, especially business-owning families, tend to confront similar challenges. The specifics differ, but parallels are legion, and if you are aware of them, you will benefit.

One of the most difficult challenges your family will face over the next one-hundred years is how to bring yourselves and one another into the business, how to accommodate each other, and how to bring out the contributions that each of you must give.

If you leave the relationship between your family and your business to its own devices, it is likely to skew off track. The result will likely be suboptimal, perhaps even disastrous.

Engagement takes work: hard, consistent, and conscious work. Relentless across the decades. Fortunately, if you approach it right, the work can be fun, satisfying, and well worth the effort. We know this to be true because we have advised and collaborated with many families who have attained this enviable position.

Conscious Commitment

Here is a high-level outline of the steps these successful families take in order to foster engagement. In the next chapter, we will dig into the details of implementation:

Step One: Understand and acknowledge the rewards of effective engagement.

Prove to yourself and your family that this *matters*, that it is worth the effort required to cultivate and sustain engagement across your family. Here is an assertion that makes the point:

> *Effective engagement will enable you to cultivate greater purpose, connection, wealth, and impact across generations.*

Purpose… connection… wealth… and impact. Who doesn't want that in their lives? But perhaps this seems too abstract, so let's boil it down into concrete, practical terms. Here's why *engagement* should matter to *you*.

If you intentionally and *effectively* incorporate your family into your business and your business into your family, you will reap the following benefits:

- You and your family will be stronger, individually and collectively.

- You will have closer relationships, and you will feel happier and more content.

- Your business will be bigger and more bountiful, so you and your family will get richer.

- You and your family will be able to make more good things happen in the world.

Please know that your business is part of your family system, whether you acknowledge it or not. If you intentionally take the time and effort to *deal* with this, then you, your people, and your business will be much better off.

Step Two: Calibrate your own desires for engagement.

You already addressed this a couple of pages ago. But just in case you glossed over the introduction to this chapter, take a moment to consider your role in your family and in your family business. Think hard.

This is your chance to understand your past, acknowledge your position in the present moment, and begin to redefine your role, if you want to. Your engagement is paramount here, the beginning of your family's transformation, if that is what you seek. Remember, put on your own oxygen mask first, before helping others.

Step Three: Take a snapshot of your current family engagement.

Put your family at center stage. What does *engagement* mean to you and to them? Who's in and who's out? How is your family doing along these lines?

Ask yourself, on a scale from 1 to 10, how engaged are you in your family's business today, and how engaged are the other branches and members of your family? You might want to grab a pencil or laptop and jot down a few names and scores. The answers may surprise you.

Once you have a baseline, you will be able to put together a plan for *cultivating* engagement.

Step Four: Digest and come to grips with three essential ideas related to engagement:

Separate but Connected

Farming vs. Hunting

Platform for Purpose

Separate But Connected

We first learned this crucial principle from our old friend Jay Hughes, whom we mentioned earlier. Hughes claims that he didn't discover the notion, but we are happy to give him credit. Here's what you need to know, in a nutshell:

> *As family members, we are permanently connected to one another. Our bonds can be strained but never completely broken. Even when we step away, we remain connected. However, at the same time, each of us is a separate individual, with independent priorities, fears, pressures, and aspirations. Each of us grapples with unique circumstances, and at some level, we must be free to come, go, and interact as we please. As members of our family, we must understand and acknowledge that for better or worse, we are in this together, but at the same time, we are each on our own path.*

The word *member* is literally important here. Your family is like a club, and every *member* belongs, with full birthrights conferred. Each of you is in. You are free to enjoy the rights and privileges of membership, and you also bear the responsibilities and accountabilities that come along with this status. But you also need the freedom to step away.

Here is what you need to know:

> Make sure your family members are welcomed into your business. At the same time, make sure they know they can get out and back in whenever they want, as long as they add value, of course. If you open the door to the cage, the birds will stay inside or roost nearby. If you lock the door, they will spend all their time biting the bars and pining to escape.

Invite them in, but don't lock them down. It should be clear to every person in your family that his or her involvement is his or her choice. Engagement is up to everyone, every day.

A Platform For Purpose

Gratitude and purpose are the wheels of the bicycle of happiness. Of course, nobody has an entirely happy life; who even knows what happiness *means*? Happiness is elusive, fleeting, and fickle at best, and it is subject to external factors from our harsh and impersonal world.

However, even accounting for all the randomness, we can make two assertions with confidence:

- When people manage to hold a sense of *gratitude* in their hearts, they are happier with *what they have*.

- When people manage to hold a sense of *purpose* in their hearts, they are happier with *who they are*.

Nothing guarantees a happy life, but if we can be grateful for what we have and enthusiastic about who we are, we are likely to float above the masses in terms of contentment, satisfaction, fulfillment, and yes, occasionally even happiness.

This is a gift we can give to ourselves and to our families. In fact, if you think about it, this is what being a family is all about:

> Family is a platform for purpose. The primary function of a family is to help its members identify, pursue, attain, and sustain their purpose in life, individually and collectively.

This is not easy, but it is possible, and for those who make it happen, it is the most rewarding thing in the world.

Farming Vs. Hunting

When families think about leadership, if they think of it at all, most of them spend their time seeking and evaluating individual candidates. This is a hunting metaphor: Go into the field with binoculars and gun. Spot some game, bag the best you can, then bring it home. It is also a recipe for conflict and mediocrity.

Rather than a shooting-and-skinning approach, families are better off when they foster engagement through cultivation.

Plant the seeds of engagement early, then continue to care for them, sincerely and consistently, across the generations. *Open the door.* Invite people in. If you're in a younger generation, open the door and push *yourself* in.

Plant the seeds of engagement, cultivate them with care, and see what happens.

This involves training, patience, constant reinforcement, tolerance for mistakes, love, and boatloads of compassion. It also takes intention and purpose, sustained and reinforced from one generation to the next. We will discuss the specifics in the following chapter.

You may feel like it's too late for your family, but it's not. We've seen so many people come together, so many families who thought their chance was gone.

If you're in a position of leadership, you'll be surprised at the reception you receive if you open this discussion. You'll be delighted by how interested people are and how much they would love to engage if you would just offer the opportunity.

If you're in a younger generation, your siblings, parents, or grandparents will welcome you into the conversation, maybe not right away, but certainly over time. In fact, deep down, this is one of their greatest dreams. They'd love to have you be engaged, but they may not know how to ask.

As Glinda the Good Witch said to Dorothy at the end of the Wizard of Oz: "You've always had the power my dear, you just had to learn it for yourself."

The Challenge Slightly Shifted

Speaking of young women like Dorothy, let's address this challenge from a different angle. We have already encountered lone-wolf entrepreneurs, people who keep their family separate and apart from their business. But the disconnect goes both ways; kids miss the boat too, all the time. Here's an example.

The family lived in a mid-sized city in New Hampshire. They had four children, three boys and a daughter, she was number three out of four. Named after her maternal grandmother, Emily was a lucky girl. Her grandfather was the founder of a manufacturing company that produced high-end plumbing fixtures, one of the major employers in town. Emily was intelligent, reasonably social, and comfortable in her own skin, despite an early preference for books over people.

As a young child, Emily had diverse interests, a handful of close friends, and an open, intense demeaner that led even casual acquaintances to pay special attention. She also had a vast imagination and an affinity for math and science, so no one was surprised when Emily became interested in medicine, even though she was only nine years old when she announced her ambition.

As she progressed through school, Emily's focus grew even tighter. Before she became a teenager, Emily began speaking with conviction about her chosen profession, glibly discussing the tradeoffs between specialties as if she was a first-year resident, not a fifth grader. Should she become a radiologist, an orthopedic hand surgeon, or a dermatologist?

Emily seemed destined for a medical career; of course, she did. Nobody, especially her father, the recently promoted CEO of the family business, ever even questioned that assumption.

In fact, not only did he refrain from questioning the notion, Emily's father *reveled* in his daughter's interest. Imagine the pride he felt. His name was Alan. He had a college education, but just barely, having spent most of his youthful time and attention with friends or working at the plant. If Emily made her dream happen, she would be the first person in the family to have earned a graduate degree, certainly the first doctor. Alan was delighted. He lavished her with attention, introducing her as his pre-pre-pre-med daughter, always with an indulging chuckle and a gentle squeeze on the shoulder.

Perhaps as a result of her intense and single-minded focus, no one ever spoke to Emily about the family business, except in the most distant, abstract terms.

Emily certainly knew about the company. Of course, she did. In fact, she loved the plant, walking there from school several times a week to do her homework in an alcove adjacent to Alan's office. Emily *worked* there too, as did her brothers, most summers and a day or two during school vacations. But this was simply a placeholder, a way station on the path to her medical career.

But Emily was secretly intrigued by the manufacturing business. You see, despite her emphatic preteen declarations, medicine wasn't her only interest. She relished her time at the plant, and she noticed things. She had ideas. Deep down, she longed to test them out. Emily resonated with the orderly progression of forging, finishing, assembly, and packing. It made intuitive sense to her, and she spent many hours in the flow, imagining and sketching out ways to improve productivity.

Emily never spoke of this interest to anyone, however, not even her father, perhaps *especially* not him. Because she was going to be a doctor, not a factory worker, right? Her early enthusiasm for medicine became a cattle chute, funneling her and her family right down the path to MD.

But a funny thing happened on the way to the hospital.

After working her brains out in high school and college, even after shadowing a doctor and then interning one summer at a pediatric clinic, it turns out that Emily *did not like* medical school. The problem was not with academics; her college grades were fine. Even organic chemistry was a breeze. She wasn't squeamish about blood either, but once she got into medical school, the lights seemed to dim, and everything turned slightly sour for some reason.

Emily didn't enjoy it, but she had so much pride. She wouldn't dream of disappointing her father, and besides, she was so enmeshed in her plans that at some level, she didn't realize she even *had* other options. So, she hung in there, gritting her teeth and saying nothing. Eventually Emily did become a doctor, but she never enjoyed it. Alan's proud glow made everything worth it though, at least at first.

Eventually, after years of discontent, Emily finally confessed her feelings to Alan during a father-daughter dinner when she was thirty-three years old. They both happened to be in Washington, DC that evening. It was a Tuesday. She was there for a medical conference, and he was visiting a distribution partner. They met for dinner at a restaurant in Georgetown, sitting on a deck overlooking the C&O Canal. It was a lovely, warm fall evening, with candlelight and a gentle, slightly musty breeze from the water below. The relaxed atmosphere and a couple glasses of wine helped Emily find the courage to confront her father.

Emily began by sharing some of her long-held questions and ideas for the business. Alan was surprised, but receptive. When he didn't reject her overtures, she took a deep breath and stunned Alan by asking him if he would ever consider letting her work in the company.

Alan was shocked and delighted. Of course, he knew that medical school had been no walk in the park, but it never is easy, and he had no idea just how deep Emily's discontent extended. He had even less inkling that she was interested in the manufacturing business. That topic had simply never come up between them. Alan welcomed her to the company with enthusiasm.

Now, ten years later, Emily is the CEO. Her transition simultaneously rejuvenated her life and turbocharged the family business. Both are growing in unexpected ways, and the family is actively cultivating the engagement of other family members.

A Personal Note: *The Importance of Purpose*

The concept of purpose is a powerful driving force for me. It provides strength when I'm tired, courage when I am afraid, and direction when I feel lost or adrift. Purpose is never fixed or permanent. Mine has evolved over time, and it has taken our family down unexpected cul-de-sacs, but looking back, there is a consistent, personal line through it all.

I have read books about purpose. I have studied the concept, discussed it often with clients, colleagues, professors, and friends.

Over the years, I have leaned upon the notion of purpose. I have even drafted a set of core values and purpose elements for my life. I bound them together in an affirmation that I regularly repeat to myself, especially when times are tough, ambiguous, or both.

I won't drag you through the affirmation in detail because it's personal, and I'm feeling kind of shy. But please know that the affirmation gives me comfort when I need it, and perhaps if you come up with one of your own, it will help you in similar fashion. Please reach out to me if you would like some help working through this process.

I *will* share my purpose with you. These elements keep me on track, and they provide immense energy when I need it:

1. *Helping my family develop and achieve their own purpose, individual and collective*

2. *Helping families succeed together in business across multiple generations*

3. *Helping individuals and families thrive beyond recovery*

4. *Building the Featherstone Holdings firm and tribe*

Element Number Three likely requires a bit of explanation. In 2014, my business partner Clyde Fossum and I raised a small investment fund from a group of families and institutional investors. We then conducted a nationwide search and acquired a business that provides specialized financial services to treatment centers and other mental health organizations. That experience opened a whole new world, introducing us to the behavioral health industry, which addresses some of the most crucial and difficult challenges our nation is facing today.

I believe that it is possible for people to not only exist *"in recovery"* from emotional and mental challenges, but to thrive *beyond* recovery. We have dedicated much of our time, attention, and other resources to helping individuals and families achieve that aspiration. In fact, our firm, Featherstone Holdings, specializes in working with behavioral health organizations that want to strengthen and scale up their operations. We even have two portfolio companies that provide teletherapy to individuals and groups.

One of my favorite aspects of working with families is helping them tease out the purpose that lies behind *their* businesses and within each of *their* hearts.

Do yourself a favor; strive for purpose. Approach the challenge with conviction. Ask the question: *Why?* Ask it of yourself, and the rest of your family. Then ask the question, *Why not?* Don't be afraid to commit, but don't commit without intention.

I will leave it there for now. Perhaps someday I will write a whole book about purpose. I might be the only one to read it, but it would be worth exploring. If you ever want to have a chat about gratitude, core values, or purpose, please reach out to us. We love this stuff.

FOOD FOR THOUGHT EXERCISE – YOU, YOURSELF, AND YOU

We're sure you've read, or at least watched, *A Christmas Carol*, by Charles Dickens. Remember Ebenezer Scrooge? Remember the ghosts who visited him on that fateful Christmas Eve? Jacob Marley, The Ghost of Christmas Past, The Ghost of Christmas Present, and The Ghost of Christmas Yet to Come.

Well, it's time to dust off that old story and apply it to yourself. This is a powerful exercise, inspired by our friend Shirzad Chamine in his wonderful book, *Positive Intelligence*.

So, go ahead and take a shot. Don't worry if takes a while. Just relax and let your imagination flow.

First, try to recall yourself as a child, preferably before you became a teenager. It might help to find a photograph. Look deeply into your own younger eyes as they look back at you from the picture or your imagination.

A lot has happened to you since then. Try to recapture the feelings, priorities, values, and dreams contained in that younger person who used to be you. Find them and project them forward to this day. Compare them to the feelings and dreams you hold in your heart right now.

Are they similar, do they rhyme? Would the younger you approve of the you who is reading these words?

Now consider a much older you, the person you will have become at the end of your life. From that perspective, look back at the you of today and the you of your childhood. What would you tell those younger people if you had the chance? What have you learned during the years that extend from today all the way to the end of your life?

Where did you go? Who did you love? What did you accomplish, and where did you fall short?

Now, from all three points of view, think about your family, family members with you today, those who are gone, and those yet unborn. What would your three selves tell each of them, and what do you hope they would tell you?

Why are you here? What is your purpose of your life? Can you imagine a collective purpose for your family? What is the purpose behind your family business?

CHAPTER 9

Implementing Engagement

We have a special place in our hearts for our agricultural clients. We have farming in our blood and dirt under our nails. Arguably, even me. I didn't grow up on a farm, but my wife Kim did, and since I was only fifteen years old when we started dating, I can assure you that I experienced plenty of cultivation firsthand.

Hot, sweaty, scabby, and itchy, she, her brother and sisters, and I spent what seemed like millions of hours standing around in fields, picking rocks, operating tractors, combines, and augers, delivering grain to bins and elevators, and running to town for parts when the machinery broke down.

We know a lot about cultivation around here, so please listen up.

Let's consider *wheat* farming for a moment. There are six basic steps to the process:

1. Prepare the soil and pray for rain.

2. Spread the seeds and pray for rain. (They call steps one and two "spring's work.")

3. Apply the chemicals required to protect the crop from plants and bugs and pray for rain.

4. Harvest the crop.

5. Sell the grain or move it into storage.

6. Get the equipment, and the financial reports, ready for next year, and pray for rain.

Like most things in this book, we've oversimplified the process, but you get the idea. And in case you are wondering, there *is* a direct link between cultivating wheat and cultivating engagement. It's not just metaphorical; your work in this area involves six steps too:

1. Offer the invitation.

2. Express purpose and values.

3. Provide a conducive environment.

4. Deliver proper training.

5. Foster empathy and trust.

6. Nurture resilience.

Lather, rinse, and repeat, repeatedly. This requires presence, persistence, and intentionality.

Offer The Invitation

The first step is easy. Simply invite people in.

This is like blood thinner; once you get started, you should never stop. You will find yourself extending invitations over and over and over again, across multiple media and formats, because people likely won't understand or believe you at first, and even when they do, they will become distracted by the events, obstacles, opportunities, and emotions they face in their own lives.

Invite them, in person and over the phone. Tweet it, add it to bedtime stories, and write it down. Buy a billboard if you need to. Everyone in your family has his or her own way of receiving messages. Adapt to each. Just make sure everyone gets the message, with frequency, or you won't be as effective as you should be.

Relax. You've got this; it is an invitation like any other. All you need is a sense of whom you are inviting and to what you are inviting them. (Once in a while, I use proper English. Don't you just love that?)

It isn't that difficult, but you need to be clear, accessible, and intentional. Here are the bare bones of the message. You supply the voice, some creativity, and plenty of repetition:

You are a member of this family, and that means you are also an owner of our business.

> *"The company belongs to all of us together. You may not actually hold shares today, but you are receiving benefits from the business, and you have an obligation to help it succeed in its mission. As an owner, you are an important part of the company's legacy and future."*

You don't have to work in the company, but you should understand the basics of what it does, why it exists, and how effective it is.

> *"I am hoping you will learn these fundamentals, and then pay attention as time goes by, so that at all times, you understand how the company is doing, what its greatest challenges and opportunities are, and what our options may be in the future."*

You will be noticed.

> *"People outside of our family will be watching you, along with the rest of our family, so they can understand what is right and important for our company and for our community."*

This is an exciting and important opportunity for you to participate in our business and to help us keep it healthy.

> *"It is also an opportunity for all of us to stay close as a family. Please pay attention and take this seriously."*

Please remember: You are a member of this family, and you always will be, no matter what.

> *"You are an owner of the company, but the choice to be active is always yours. You are welcome to come close or stay away. I sincerely hope that you decide to be a part of this great organization we are building together."*

Please note: If you are not in position to extend the invitation, if instead, you seek to become engaged in your family business, simply swap the word *you* for the words *I* or *us* in the above framework. Invite *yourself* in. Declare your interest and your ownership. See what happens. We bet you'll be pleasantly surprised.

Express Purpose And Values

If you don't already have your purpose and core values nailed down, we recommend that you begin doing so right away. These elements will also come into play when we discuss the *clarity building block*.

If you craft and deploy them properly, purpose and core values will drill directly to the heart and soul of your business, enabling you to attract, evaluate, and inspire every person and organization that comes into contact with it, inside and outside the family.

As mentioned above, at Featherstone, we are purpose *fanatics*. Few things are more important to a company than the reason it exists and the principles for which it stands.

We typically encourage people to express their company's purpose through a clear, concise, and compelling mission statement.

Most corporate mission statements are long, boring diatribes, full of jargon and devoid of meaningful content. That is *not* what you want.

Short, sweet, and powerful; that's the ticket.

In our opinion, your mission statement should boil down to one simple sentence. Everyone, in your family and in your company, should buy into it, and they should all be able to recite it easily from memory. Here are some examples from clients with whom we have worked:

To relentlessly advocate for people who need treatment.

We provide value and foundation stability to businesses, homes, and families.

To change our industry by eliminating corrosion in civic water systems.

Leading teens and their families back to a full life, with resilience, hope, and love.

To protect what matters… the physical, emotional, and financial wellbeing of our clients and their people.

Transforming Lives through Sustainable Outcomes

To enable individuals and their families to thrive beyond recovery.

Your mission statement should express your purpose in the simplest possible terms. It should strike a chord within the hearts of all true believers. When that doesn't happen, either your mission statement isn't clear enough, or that person should *leave*. Simple as that.

Core values should also be clear and simple. They need to be deeply true, not just window dressing, and there can't be too many of them. No more than ten, to be sure, and five is better than eight.

These are not just words. This needs to be *real*. You need to mean it, and you, your family, and your company need to live it. That means every day, or it will become a meaningless joke. Literally, your employees, your customers, and your children will *laugh* at you if you don't live up to your mission and core values, so be careful.

Get your family together and nail these down. Start with your purpose, then from that, compose your one-sentence mission statement. Next, identify and describe your core values, one by one. Many exercises and fun games exist to guide you and your family through this process. If you are interested in learning more, please call us or visit our web site.

Provide A Conducive Environment

Lip service is such a trite and tired phrase, and so is Mom's apple pie, but like the iceberg metaphor, these epigrams persist because there is so much truth behind them.

Plenty of families talk about engagement. It is *easy* to talk about engagement, and hard to argue against it. *Who wouldn't want to be informed? Who wouldn't want to be involved?* But saying it and making it happen are two very different things.

The best way to start is by formalizing the invitation by providing the venue for discussion. Invite your family members to an in-person meeting. If you can't manage that for some reason, set up a video meeting or a conference call. It may seem awkward at first to introduce this level of formality to your family dynamic, but it will make a considerable difference. We know this to be true because we facilitate meetings like this on a regular basis.

Rather than just *wanting* to be engaged, people will *feel* engaged, and they will commit more fully to your process as it develops.

After the initial kickoff meeting, we recommend quarterly video meetings or conference calls, with a once a year, in-person gathering. We love to facilitate family meetings and retreats, and we would be happy to pass along some complimentary materials you can use to bring yours to life. Please reach out if you are interested in pursuing this.

Deliver Proper Training

Imagine a college classroom, full of bright-eyed students, but without a specific topic, syllabus, or textbook. It wouldn't necessarily spell disaster; with a smart teacher and willing pupils, there could certainly be meaningful dialogue. Perhaps people would even take value away from the discussion. But more likely, the kids would not receive a fair trade for their tuition money. You need a core curriculum for your family and your business.

If people are going to make the effort to engage, they will need to absorb and become familiar with your core curriculum over time. It doesn't all have to spew forth in the first meeting, but during the first nine to twelve months, you should introduce your family members to all the basic elements they will need to know in order to be on track as informed owners.

Every family is unique, and so is every family business. But, given that grain of salt, here is an initial list of fundamental elements you should consider:

1. The story of the company, its founding, and its history, from the beginning until today

2. The purpose and core values of the family and the company

3. The primary customer groups served by the company

4. The main products and services sold by the company

5. The key objectives of the business, financial, strategic, and tactical

6. Scientific and/or product development concepts and targets

7. Some of the main obstacles and opportunities the company faces today

8. Storm clouds and rainbows on the distant horizon

9. Competitors and examples of companies you are trying to emulate

10. Organizational chart

11. Key managers, family and otherwise, along with their roles and their backgrounds

12. A list of the most important customers, along with explanations of what drives them

The list goes on, but this is a good start. Of course, you need to be careful to approach this information in an age appropriate way, considering confidentiality and other information management guidelines. Nobody is ready to hear everything all at once, and that's okay, because you have plenty of time. This is a long journey. For now, simply encourage people to take the first step.

If some of your elements are not clear or formalized enough— purpose, core values, organizational chart, and strategic overview, for example—family meetings are an excellent forum for refining them. Pick one key topic for each meeting. If you have the time and energy, distribute initial materials ahead of the meeting. It may feel clunky at first, but as you gain experience together, these meetings will become engaging and productive.

Foster Empathy And Trust

Okay, now we've come to the hard part, at least for most families. People have written many books about trust, the importance of it, how to earn it, and how to *exploit* it. Some of these books inspire hope, and some inspire fear. We have read many of them, and we have developed a system of our own for evaluating and distinguishing between the various levels of trust that define the boundaries of our relationships.

There isn't room in this book for a full treatment of trust, but you can visit our web site if you want to dig in deeper. For now, we will simply make a few observations and encourage you to take these topics seriously.

In a perfect world, we would be able to seamlessly earn the trust of others, and in turn, we would be willing to trust them. But alas, the world isn't perfect, and neither are we. Even when it comes to family, perhaps *especially* when it comes to family, trust can loom insurmountable, like Mount Everest on a dark and windy day.

But we must make the attempt, we must scale that mountain, perhaps with the aid of oxygen, strong ropes, provisions, and quick-witted sherpas. If we remain isolated down in the flat lands, we will never reach a view that is worth the climb.

Now that we've managed to stretch *that* metaphor to the breaking point, here is one more tug: *If Mount Everest represents the pinnacle of trust, than empathy is the basecamp.*

Trust begins with empathy. If you don't consciously try to understand the other guy and his or her position, you will never earn their trust, and you won't be able to trust *them* either. Like many of the other concepts in our book, this one is infinite in scope and depth, and our commitment to keeping things short and sweet precludes proper treatment. We apologize for this, and to compensate, we have posted essays on both trust and empathy on our web site. You are welcome to dig in, and we encourage you to do so.

We will leave you with one additional tidbit here. In addition to individual empathy, strive for generational empathy. Try to listen and understand the situation from the perspectives of the other generations who are involved in your family and your business. We recognize four generations:

1. Senior   Ages 60 +

2. Prime   Ages 25 to 59

3. Next-Gen   Ages 12 to 24

4. Puppies   Ages 4 to 11

Each of these generations has its own perspectives, aspirations, pressures, and insecurities. It is so easy to look at our family, our company, and the world only through the lens of our own generation, but when we do, we fail to perceive important clues that can help us relate and bring one another closer.

Okay, one more thing about trust:

> If you truly trust one another, then conflict is a good thing. You can safely embrace it, and it will lead you to the promised land.

Believe it or not, we spend much of our time with clients fostering healthy conflict, within their families and their companies. And when we're not doing that, you will likely find us working with families to transform their conflict from destructive to healthy.

We don't eliminate conflict; we *harness* it. We seek to *embrace* conflict, and when we can do so, we know we have achieved high levels of empathy and trust.

Nurture Resilience

This last step represents the culmination of every other aspect of engagement, and it spreads back out again to each. The six steps represent an endless cycle, one that should get stronger and better with every revolution of the flywheel.

The invitation is always there, open, and frequently expressed. Purpose and Core Values are clear, concise, compelling, and deeply *true*. We have a safe and consistent environment that fosters communication, and within that environment, there is a steady flow of information that conveys the training required to keep all the owners up to speed. Finally, there is plenty of empathy, listening and understanding, which results in deep levels of trust, deep enough, in fact, to sustain and channel healthy conflict.

If you bring these elements together, consistently, with intention and integrity, you will be on the right track. Then, if you sprinkle in liberal amounts of flexibility, open-mindedness, and tolerance of mistakes, you will produce family members who are capable of withstanding pressure, uncertainty, fear, and adversity. People who can fall, repeatedly, only to get up and keep on fighting each time. People with *grit*.

You and your family will become strong and resilient enough to succeed together for a hundred years or more.

Family is a platform for *Purpose*, and *Engagement* provides a solid base for the platform.

Personal Note: *I Never Knew*

It bothers me when people tell me that their children are not interested in their business. Especially if they express this thought in an offhand way, as if that's just the way things are, as if they had no role in that lack of interest.

Don't get me wrong. I understand that kids are often, if not usually, disinterested in the family business. Heck, even *my* kids aren't interested in my business.

What bothers me is not the lack of interest on the part of the kids, it's *parent's* lack of interest that gets me down. Remember, this is a long process of cultivation. Casually tossing out the comment that 'my kids just don't care' is like a farmer saying: 'I don't have a crop this year' after having failed to plant any seeds in the spring.

Get them involved now; it is never too late. They don't have to work in the business. Perhaps that ship has sailed already, at least for a while, but they can learn *about* the business, take active roles as stakeholders or owners. This business is a member of the family; don't let people off the hook without at least trying to reel them in.

Generating engagement requires leadership and focused intention. You can do it, though, and it's worth every ounce of effort. The human, social, enterprise, and financial capital you will receive will carry you forward across the generations.

I know about this from a firsthand perspective. As you recall, I was a member of a business-owning family. Nobody ever invited me in, and I never tried to open the door for myself. What a wasted opportunity.

I'm not griping about that; everything has turned out very well for us, but please don't tell me that your next generation is not interested if you have never pushed hard to make them informed or invited them in. You can make so much happen if you try.

By the way, I could have tried harder too, and shame on me for not doing so.

FOOD FOR THOUGHT EXERCISE – AN ENGAGEMENT MESSAGE FOR YOUR FAMILY

What if it was up to you, only you, to bring your family together? How would you convince them to sit up and pay attention? How would you resolve the conflicts, perceived slights, and grudges, many of which arose so long ago?

Well, you know what? You *are* responsible for bringing your family together. That is, if you're willing to accept the challenge. Bringing them together along family dimensions and around the business.

As we mentioned at the beginning of this book, stories are a powerful medium for engaging people, for uniting them, for conveying important and complex messages.

Close your eyes and try to imagine a narrative that you could use to strengthen the engagement of your family. Work hard for a few moments. Try to make it simple, concise, and compelling. I bet you can do it, and you and your family will be glad you did.

CHAPTER 10

The Principles Of Clarity

It's time to get clear about clarity. We believe that most failures in business, and many of the heartbreaks that strike families, stem from a lack of clarity. People don't understand what they stand for, why they do what they do, who should do what, what each person wants and receives, when to quit, when to dig in.

The trouble is, most of the time, with rare exception, people just don't *get* it. You think they should, but they don't, not unless things are spelled out, *clearly* and *directly*. If you've ever been married or in a long-term relationship, you'll know how frustrating and ineffective it is when someone expects you to read their mind, and if we're honest, we'll admit that it almost never works out when we expect others to read ours.

Life shouldn't be that way; but it is, *especially in business.*

Sure, there are a few gifted chefs out there who can whip together a meal without recipes, and there are plenty of folks who are so familiar with their regular dishes that they can crank out solid meals every time, but when it comes to breaking new ground, when it comes down to building something for the future or coordinating complex processes and systems across distributed groups, when it comes to making seafood lasagna and German chocolate cake from scratch for the first time, without clarity, things usually break down, or they don't taste very good in the end.

Let's mix some more metaphors, shall we? As we mentioned before, when people encounter a deep fog or snowstorm on the highway, they can't perceive the center line or guard rails, so they drift between the fence posts, making slow progress at best, scraping off their rearview mirrors and even deploying airbags under extreme circumstances.

Are things any different from within your family or its business? We are all operating in a fog.

The clarity building block exists to eliminate, or at least mitigate, this problem. Clarity involves both the family and the business, and in fact, it builds a bridge between the two.

Rodney's Clarity Story

Here is a story that animates some of the principles of clarity.

Rodney, the founder of a company called FasTron, had five children. He went into business for himself when he was a young man, back in 1972. Rodney's business involved distributing fasteners. "What the heck are fasteners?" you might ask. Well, you probably have a few on your person right now. Buttons, zippers, Velcro; and those are just the wearable bits.

What about all the screws, bolts, nuts, washers, standoffs, rivets, grommets, cotters, staples, and anchors that surround you every day? Microscopic to massive; plastic, rubber, galvanized steel, and precision-engineered surgical titanium. There's a whole *universe* of fasteners out there. Don't get us started. We *loved* working with these guys; had *no* idea that something so mundane on the surface could be so cool once you know what to look for.

Rodney originally approached us because he feared that Chinese knockoff vendors were in position to eat FasTron's lunch. He was right, but that's not what this story is about. This is about clarity, specifically about Rodney's oldest child, a son named Raymond, and his little brother Roger, separated in birth order by two of their three sisters.

By the way, if you're wondering why only the boys are featured here, it's because only the boys had anything to do with the business. Don't ask us why. We don't like that old, tired song any more than you do.

Father and sons; different names, same initials. Rodney was always Rodney. Most of the time, Raymond was Ray, and Roger was Roger.

Remember Emily from the last chapter? She's the one who went to medical school only to realize that what she really wanted was to work in her family's business? Well, Ray's story involves medicine too, but his is the inverse of Emily's.

Rodney always knew that Ray would take over the business someday. So did Ray, and so did everyone else. No question. Ray started working at the company, light duty, when he was only nine years old, summers and weekends. Roger was just a toddler back then.

Rodney groomed Ray every step of the way. Even when he was a kid, Ray would accompany Rodney to conferences, trade shows, and sales calls. He looked so cute in his little mohair suit. Young Ray became a fastener fanatic; you might say that instead of elbows and tendons, he had hinges, bungie cords, and u-joints. Eventually, Ray went to college, a local school, where he studied business management.

Raymond worshipped his father, and he loved the business too. Why wouldn't he? It was his destiny. Everybody took that for granted. Ray was an expert, and FasTron was his sandbox, his refuge from an early age. Ray felt comfortable there, in control, fully in charge of his faculties and his skills.

After college, Ray joined the business fulltime. Worked his way toward the top, striving to outperform everybody else because he was Rodney's son. He knew he had to push it in order to earn his proper place in the eyes of the team.

Bottom line: Ray did everything he could to get in, but you know what? The whole time, underneath it all, a tiny corner of his mind *burned* to get out.

Raymond had always been a big reader. From a young age, he was attracted to science and math, and he enjoyed conceptualizing complex systems. Ray used to watch medical shows and movies on TV, and he loved the early Michael Creighton novels that featured physicians valiantly solving crimes and fighting epidemics.

You see, like our old friend Emily from the last chapter, Raymond was fascinated by medicine, ever since he was a little kid. But whereas Emily was free to pursue that interest, Ray never even got to ask the question out loud; he was fastened to the fastener business, with no way out.

That was not a problem at first. Ray had FasTron, and he launched into his career with extreme focus. He even spent his free time dreaming up new promotions and searching for innovative products they could license. It was a happy time for Ray; he was in the flow and learning so much. But after a few years of this, Ray noticed that his father Rodney wasn't letting him off the leash, and he wasn't revealing many thoughts and plans either.

Ray was still selling like crazy, busy and productive every day, but he started to chafe, simultaneously pushing against his father and drifting away. Ray began feeling that he was simply a character in his *father's* narrative, not the family business leader he always assumed he would be. Prince Charles all over again.

After this virus of doubt infected his psyche, Ray's daydreams began to change, from "How do we sell more this quarter?" to "Could I have been a doctor? Should I have been? How would my life be different today?"

Eventually, Ray was spending most of his creative cycles flaring up in temper tantrums or dreaming about breaking free from the business he loved so much. It just didn't feel like *his* anymore. He was still working all day at the shop, but his mind, often beneath the surface, was busy digging escape tunnels in his imagination.

But wait, *what about Roger?*

Well, Roger was six years younger than Ray, and Ray was Roger's hero, always had been; Spiderman, Superman, and Bill Nye the Science Guy, all wrapped up into one big brother package. All Roger wanted was to be where Ray was, to do what Ray could do.

So, Roger became a fastener fanatic too, but he was quiet about it, as he was about so many things. When he was old enough, Roger simply followed Ray to work and never left.

Roger watched as the heir apparent, big brother Ray, tried his best to become the public face of FasTron. Ray was the outside guy, and over time, he began trying to call the shots as their father began pulling back. But Ray got nowhere with that approach, because he didn't have enough insight or authority.

This is when lack of clarity really started to rear its triangular-shaped, rattlesnake head. You see, Rodney, father and founder, may have been pulling back his hours, but he refused to transfer visibility or control.

Rodney was not ready to transition, and just like in the old days, he kept everything to himself. It's not that he was consciously keeping secrets. It's just that, ever since the beginning of FasTron, and perhaps even before, Rodney had simply kept his own counsel. He carried a sophisticated structure of priorities, plans, and worries in his mind, and there it stayed. Locked up tight. He constantly thought about these things, ruminated, picked at the worries and plans as if they were a rash or a bunch of old sores. It was just part of his existence, and it didn't occur to him to proactively share it with others.

Besides, this was still his company. Rodney maintained 100 percent ownership of the business, and he was not ready to let that go. In Rodney's mind he held onto this assumption: "Raymond and Roger may think they should be calling the shots, but that won't be happening any time soon."

Rodney wasn't consciously pushing the boys away from his business. The information was always there for them, if they wanted to ask. He was simply running things the way he always had. Rodney saw his sons working hard, and that made him smile inside; this is exactly what he had envisioned all those years ago. Someday, too far in the future to contemplate, Rodney would hand the reigns over to Ray and fulfill their mutual destiny. But for now, everything was safe and sound in Rodney's prefrontal cortex.

Occasionally, Rodney would mention the fact that the kids would inherit; "This will be yours someday," but nobody knew when, or even *what* that meant.

Everything was vague, including the financials. During and after a bad month, Rodney would stomp through the office, griping about margins and all the money he had invested so his kids could have a nice life, but Ray and Roger were too busy to dig into the details, and "the girls" didn't even have a clue, so everyone felt whipsawed, based upon Rodney's moods, health, and level of anxiety.

Each of the boys reacted differently to this lack of clarity.

Ray continued to check out, more and more over time, swapping focus for diversion and discontent. He became an avid fly fisherman, spending days at a time standing in rivers. He collected vintage cars. For a while, he became a running fanatic. He made long-shot, half-baked investments. He ran for the state senate and lost. He also cheated on his wife, ignored his kids, drank too much, *yelled* too much, and eventually let himself slide into a state of serious mental, physical, and emotional despair.

Little brother Roger had a different reaction; he simply put his head down and worked harder. By his mid-thirties, Roger had become the inside guy, migrating eventually to a position that you might have called head of operations, if things like that had been spelled out. Roger took home his paycheck, which he vaguely understood was smaller than Ray's. In exchange, he poured his heart into the operation, and he continued to worship his big brother, although he had begun to feel a nascent sense of resentment.

Since the organizational structure wasn't clear, and since by this time Ray and Rodney were frequently galivanting away from the office, employees, customers, and suppliers naturally gravitated to Roger. In his quiet way, Roger stepped up and did the best he could, cranking it out fourteen hours per day or more. Eventually, everything settled upon Roger's broad and capable shoulders.

Roger did fine for a time. But occasionally, Rodney or Ray would get inspired, barge back into the office, and mess everything up. This caused tremendous heartache for everyone involved, especially Roger. Resentment eventually built up to the breaking point. Sales plunged, and so did profit margins. Rodney blamed this on the Chinese, and Ray blamed it on Rodney. Roger was simply pissed off.

The brothers, Ray and Roger, began fighting, *really fighting*, for the first time in their lives. They felt a helpless sense of dread while they worked, like the members of that string quartet, making beautiful music on the deck of the Titanic, as the stern of the ship sunk lower and lower toward the sea.

By the time Rodney reached out to our firm, things were looking grim. Roger had received an employment offer from a heavy-equipment dealer across town, and he had announced that he was seriously considering it. An Asian company really *was* making a bid for several of FasTron's biggest customers. Ray was separated from his wife, and Rodney was fit to be tied.

We recognized this sorry state of affairs for what it really was, having seen this movie so many times in the past with other families. This problem stemmed from lack of clarity, not offshore competition. We knew what had to be done, and we convinced "The Three Rs" to commit to a weekend retreat in order to begin to stop the bleeding.

It took more than a weekend, of course, but you would be surprised what you can accomplish when people sincerely strive for clarity and alignment. During that initial three days, we planted the seeds of a revitalized organization that would feature true transparency, one which would include clearly defined roles and responsibilities, straightforward and fair compensation, and a multi-year transition plan.

Within a few weeks, we developed a Scalability RoadMap bolstered by a clear organizational structure, consistent financial reporting, publicly stated goals and metrics, and genuinely interactive leadership team meetings. It took about a year of concerted effort, but things eventually turned around. As clarity set in, the family and the company became unified and resilient once again.

You'll be happy to know that the boys also managed to salvage their relationship. Raymond caught himself in time. He spent three years regrouping. He repaired broken relationships, resumed reasonable exercise, cut back on harmful things, focused on good things, and recommitted himself to the business.

To everyone's surprise, Roger became the CEO, but no one was surprised to see him succeed. One of the shining lights of the business became a new division, launched and run by Ray, that produced and distributed medical fasteners and disposables.

There continue to be challenges, frustrations, and plenty of conflict, of course. There always are. But once they cleaned their lenses and illuminated the shadows, the wounds started to heal and their path became navigable once again. Today, G3, the third generation, is working in the company. We believe this organization could continue to thrive for the next one hundred years or more.

The Clarity Lifestyle

Clarity isn't just a choice; it is a philosophy, it is a commitment, it is a *lifestyle*.

Some people seem to thrive on ambiguity and compartmentalization. Others cut corners, shade the truth, and manipulate others, justified by the perspective that knowledge is power. Those are proven strategies, we reluctantly admit. Many people "succeed" in that way, that is, if their definition of *success* includes only money and power.

If your definition of success *also* includes robust relationships, multi-generational resilience, human capital maximization, and sincere social impact, then you're not going to achieve it behind a smoke screen.

As with the other concepts in this book, the notion of clarity is infinitely rich, but we don't have time to fully explore it. Here are the four principles we consider most elemental.

Principle #1: Clear Expectations

When things are clear, people know what to expect. This is such a simple and obvious concept, but why is it so *hard* to achieve?

Do yourself a favor, try like hell to live your life, both with your family and in your business, in such a way that the people around you know what to expect, and nurture an environment that enables you to know what you can expect from them.

That's a pretty solid definition of heaven right there. It's a never-ending quest, but well worth the effort. Expectations are the cornerstones of clarity, and clarity will set you free.

Expectation setting involves consistent behavior, clearly expressed, along with thoroughly communicated values, deliverables, goals, milestones, success measures, timing, costs, and other results of your work and actions.

Principle #2: Clear Standards

The first cousins of expectations are standards. In fact, standards reflect and produce expectations. In that sense, calling them out may seem redundant, but it's helpful to consider standards in a separate light of their own. Standards can be physical, temporal, behavioral, ethical, and aesthetic, among other things.

Consciously set standards, for yourself, for your family, for your company, and for your friends. Set them, publicize them, and track them. Commit your standards to writing, and communicate them with clarity, every chance you get. Your standards will keep you on track, and they will serve you well in many additional ways.

Principle #3: Clear Ground Rules

These first three principles may feel to some like nested Russian dolls, and they do rhyme closely with one another. However, as with standards, it is useful to consider the concept of ground rules as a separate principle, because people are so hungry to know where their boundaries are, in their personal lives and their work lives.

This includes behavioral norms and taboos, compensation criteria, hierarchical reporting protocols, and myriad other relationship dynamics. Make the rules clear and consistent. Calibrate them with your Core Values. Post them and discuss them. Make them transparent, and you will run a much tighter ship.

Principle #4: Clear Focus

Few things are more crucial or beneficial in business than focus. Knowing what to do, and even more important, what *not* to do, makes all the difference in the world.

As with purpose, the challenge and discipline of focus extend from each of us as individuals through to our collective actions in groups and organizations. Without clarity, you cannot have meaningful focus, and without focus, you cannot move mountains.

We have developed many processes, exercises, tools, and documents to help you find, express, and stick with your focus. Please visit our web site if you want to dig in deeper.

The next chapter will show us how to harness the principles of clarity in order to create and implement practical documents and disciplines that will streamline progress for our families and our companies.

A Personal Note: *Waiting Tables in College*

Being a waiter taught me many things. Mexican, Asian, Italian: You name it, I served it. That, along with federally subsidized student loans, is how I paid my tuition and financed my first company.

Waiting tables was one of the hardest jobs I ever had, and I've done *plenty* of hard jobs. If you have never waited tables for a living, you may have chuckled when you read that claim. But if you *have* been a waitron, you will know that I speak the truth.

I defy you to juggle sixteen tables for seven hours on a busy Saturday night. Be careful, however; the experience could take *years* off your life.

Why am I going down this rabbit hole when we're trying to keep the book nice and short? Because waiting tables is *all about* clarity and expectations. That's the biggest lesson I learned from the restaurant business, and in fact, it is one of the most important insights I absorbed during all my college years.

Life is all about setting and fulfilling expectations. If you understand that, and you can make it happen, then you will receive $200 per night in tips. If not, you will quickly flame out.

If the kitchen's backed up, let your customers know, clearly and without hesitation. If they over cooked the steak, or under cooked the eggs, 'fess up right away. Tell them what you're going to do to fix the situation, then do it. Simple as that.

If they know what to expect, you'll be surprised by how tolerant restaurant customers can be. They are there to have a good time, not to wonder what's going on. They're probably hangry already, and they will get even more nervous and irritable if they don't feel informed and in control.

Manage their expectations. You might need to bring them extra bread or chips; you might even have to slip them a free drink or dessert now and then, but they will put up with almost anything if they understand what to expect. Remember that. It will, um, *serve* you well, in the restaurant of life.

That's one of my key disciplines when it comes to working with boards of directors, venture capital investors, employees, clients, and family members. I learned this the hard way, multiple times: let them know what to anticipate, keep them informed, and do your best to exceed their expectations.

I still have plenty of headaches with boards, investors, and employees, I'm sorry to say, but it would be even worse if my experience as a waiter hadn't forced me to internalize the bedrock value of setting and fulfilling expectations.

Oh, by the way, here's a bonus waiter lesson that I continue to apply in my business life, nearly forty years after the fact. I call it *The Coffee Test*. Whenever I'm recruiting a new employee or client, I pose questions and set up scenarios that will help me determine the following:

> *If my candidate was a waiter or waitress on a frantically busy weekend, what would happen if one of his or her customers ordered the last cup of coffee in the pot? Would this person pause long enough to prepare a new pot for his or her colleagues, or would they simply fill their client's cup and run back into the dining room, leaving an empty, burning pot for the next guy?*

Think about that for a moment. It may sound trivial, but if you have ever waited tables, you know it's a real thing. That line of inquiry has guided me many times as I have hired and fired people throughout the years.

FOOD FOR THOUGHT EXERCISE – *NOTES AND MIRRORS*

Let's look at your level of clarity. In your imagination or in your notebook, make three lists.

List #1: External Factors

What is murky in your life? Record any situations, relationships, behaviors, and implications, from your personal life and your professional life, that feel cloudy, inconsistent, or unfair. Just do a brain dump, in free-form style. You can organize it later.

You will probably find this hard going at first, but I bet you will warm to the task and surprise yourself by identifying unclear dynamics that you hadn't even noticed before.

When you're satisfied with the initial list, sit back and review it. Then tighten or reorganize it if you like. Take as many passes as you want until you feel like you have a meaningful list. Then look carefully at each entry. Jot down the role you play in the lack of clarity behind each one.

List #2: Contributing Behaviors And Attitudes

From that initial level of understanding, you will create your second list, a list of your behaviors and attitudes that inhibit clarity. Look in the mirror, be honest with yourself, and write down the things you do and think that fog the looking glass of your life.

List #3: Clarification Outline

This list will be short, but super important. Identify two to four situations that you can and *will* clarify in the next sixty days. Pick some items from list number one and promise yourself that you will make them better. You might also want to include a target date and some action steps or milestones for each one so you can lock in the commitment and ensure a solid sense of direction.

CHAPTER 11

Implementing Clarity

I f you inject more clarity into your family and into your business, then your life will be a better. Faster, easier, richer, and more satisfying all around. We *promise*.

Clarity illuminates the dark corners of your family and your business. It reveals direction, sets expectations, specifies standards, guides behavior, and tightens focus. It is a *miracle* drug.

So how do we conjure up clarity for ourselves, our families, our relationships, and our companies?

Well, as with *engagement*, this is a life-long process. We are about to describe a set of disciplines, called the six clarities. They will enable you to polish the lenses of your life, and here they are, all in one list:

1. *Vision*
2. *Transformation Plan*
3. *Priorities*
4. *Organization*
5. *Compensation*
6. *Control*

Each of the six clarities applies at multiple levels, including yourself, your family, and your business. We will present them primarily from the perspective of your business, but as you read through this chapter, please try to keep each of the other levels in mind.

Vision

Vision is related to, but different from, purpose. The distinction between the two is subtle but important. Purpose refers to w*hy* something exists; vision refers to w*hat* it will become. Purpose refers in general to the *type* of work we do, and the kind of results we seek. Vision refers to how much of that work we will do, what we will specifically deliver, and what we aim to accomplish as a result.

Let's illustrate with an example.

In the next chapter, we will tell the story of a wonderful organization called Dakota Teen Triumph, an outpatient treatment center for adolescents who are struggling with emotional and behavioral issues. One of the key focus areas of our firm involves the behavioral health industry, and we are especially proud to be working with this group.

We previously presented the mission statement for Dakota Teen Triumph: *Leading teens and their families back to a full life, with resilience, hope, and love.*

That statement expresses the purpose of Dakota Teen Triumph (DTT), but it does not spell out the vision.

An organization with a similar mission could have a single, small storefront in New Bedford, MA. It could have twenty-seven locations across the Midwest, or it could have a massive online operation, headquartered in Silicon Valley. A company with that mission could provide residential care, outpatient therapy, wilderness programs, video-based teletherapy, or subscription-only educational materials. Each of those approaches is legitimate and could fulfill the mission.

Is this a bread box, a breadbasket, or a bread truck? That's what vision will tell us; clarity demands it.

A solid vision statement for DTT will specify the services they intend to provide, along with the scale at which they intend to provide it, at a, specified point in the future.

This literally is a kind of *vision*, an image or snapshot of where the company will be in a specified amount of time. Here is an example statement that could express the vision for Dakota Teen Triumph:

> *In five years, we will have between fifteen and twenty outpatient centers in the Midwestern United States, consistently serving an average of fifty teens for three months each. That means we will be serving between 3,000 and 4,000 teens and their families per year, providing them a combination of day treatment, intensive outpatient, general outpatient, and family counseling services.*

Whew! Is that clear, or what? A specific vision everyone can grab onto, showing us exactly where the organization will be in five years.

Of course, the only certain thing about a vision is that it won't be entirely accurate, but that's okay. It's the *directionality* that counts. A vision, well-crafted and eagerly pursued, will provide focus, energy, and alignment to everyone involved with the organization.

Transformation Plan

A transformation plan starts with our current position, then it takes our vision as an input, and it lays out the work required to get us there. It presents a step-by-step course of action that will lead us from where we are today to where we want to be on a specific date in the future.

This is nothing new. Plans like this have been around ever since those cavemen we mentioned earlier realized that there might be more to life than clubbing one another and running away from saber-toothed tigers. Variously called strategic plans, business plans, implementation plans, and many other things, they are the bane of MBA students and business managers everywhere.

They are also essential ingredients for clarity.

We call them transformation plans because they describe the steps and priorities required to *transform* our organization. The Scalability RoadMap, mentioned earlier, represents a high-level, simplified version of such a plan.

We wish we had a whole book's worth of space to describe the ins and outs of preparing, adjusting, and managing with a transformation plan. Please let us know if you would like additional guidance in this area. We will gladly send you some helpful materials.

Priorities

Priorities and plans: When we were kids, we got so sick of hearing about priorities and plans. Well, this may not be what *you* want to hear either, but *machines* run the world, and *priorities* run the machines.

There is a silver lining, however. The great thing about priorities, if you can bring yourself to embrace and stick with them, is that they do make life easier, and they accelerate the progress toward your vision.

We have developed a multi-level approach to priority setting. We'll present it from the perspective of your business, but please remember that this technique also applies to your individual priorities and the collective priorities of your family.

Based on the notion that anything worth doing is worth doing right, we strictly limit the number of our key priorities. We call them T-Goals. The *T* stands for *Tremendous* and *Target*. At any given time, your company should have one, two, or at the most, three T-Goals, and they should be *big*. T-Goals generally extend for about twelve months, but that's not a hard and fast rule. They can be shorter or longer in duration.

As with transformation plans, we cannot claim to have invented the concept of managing through focused goals. Jim Collins and Jerry Porras call them BHAGs (*Big Hairy Audacious Goals*), Andy Grove and John Doerr call them OKRs (*Objectives and Key Results*), and the folks at FranklinCovey call them WIGs (*Wildly Important Goals*). Same wine, different bottles, but essential. No surprise, we like our version best.

One of the aspects of which we particularly appreciate is the D-Goal. The D stands for *department* or *direct*. As you can imagine, under this system, all the departments within your organization would craft a set of D-Goals, each of which rolls up to, and thus enables the organization to achieve, its T-Goals. A properly executed set of T-Goals, along with effective supporting D-Goals, will guide the organization from its current position to the promised land described in your transformation plan.

In the end, it doesn't matter what you call them. Please, just get your priorities straight. If you would like more help in this area, visit our website for some cool supporting documents.

Organization

Most family business owners make the mistake of building their organization chart around *people*, often family members. That's not true. Most family business owners don't even bother to create an organizational chart at all. But the ones who *do*, typically draw them with specific individuals in mind. This is the *wrong* approach.

A scalable organizational chart will be built around *positions*, not people. Once you understand and define the positions, what they are supposed to do, to whom they report, and how they relate to one another, then you are ready to insert specific names into each box.

If you follow this approach, you will inevitably end up with individuals whose names appear in multiple boxes. That is fine. Over time, as the company grows, multi-box folks will be able to tighten their focus, shedding some of their boxes as the company hires more people. Here is an example of a position-based organizational structure. With a small bit of tweaking, a chart like this could accommodate companies ranging from nine to over a hundred employees.

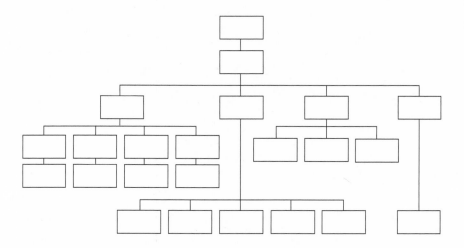

Remember, clarity is the objective here. A person-based organizational chart will bring you opacity and heartache. A well-crafted, position-based organizational chart will set you free to scale the business.

Compensation

This is a tough one, which is why most people gloss over compensation and do such a bad job of dealing with the dynamics that surround it. Once again, we are skimming the surface of a tremendously deep subject, but it is crucial that we all understand and acknowledge the importance of clear communication here.

First things first. We are not suggesting that you somehow publicize what everyone is getting paid. That is not the point at all; and in fact, we believe that would be a recipe for strife and disaster.

We *are* suggesting, however, that you clarify and communicate compensation as much as you can. There may be opportunities to share some compensation details within departments or across group-based bonus and profit sharing, but that's not our main point.

At the very least, everyone in the organization, and everyone in your family, should *clearly* understand how they make their own money, what they need to do to receive it, and how much they can expect at every level of performance. They should also have a general, but not specific, idea of how it works for others. If you illuminate the dark corners, you eliminate much of the anxiety.

This sounds simple and obvious, but if it's so obvious, why the heck do so many families and businesses screw it up? It is quite difficult to nail compensation, but your life, and the performance of your business, will be much better if you manage to do so.

Control

The buck stops *where*? And with *whom*? People need to know, and *you* need to be clear and consistent.

Epic novels, movies, TV series, and even *empires* have been built around this question. Answer it wrong, and you will find yourself in the hurt bag. Do it right, and you will be in position to flourish and grow.

Let us recall that the focus of this chapter is clarity. Corporate control, influence, and decision making are the blood vessels of your organization, and they are also the lifeblood of your family. If you tangle them or plug them up too much, the patient will gasp, and perhaps even expire.

Control ultimately comes down to ownership, and in family business, this can resemble a minefield, because it is impossible to know where every expectation, resentment, and conflict is buried. Many, if not all, of your family members feel connected, to one another and to your business, and many of them also feel a sense of entitlement, with expectations that stem from goodness knows where. Since that is the case, you will be so much better off if you can eliminate the ambiguity.

A good organizational chart, with clear guidelines for compensation will help, but we also need clear governance, for the family and for the business. Many proven structures and documents exist to help you think this through. They do *not* have to be extensive and complicated, and properly deployed, they *will* enable you to achieve solid corporate and family governance.

Here is a list of common corporate governance elements:

1. Board of Directors
2. Board of Advisors
3. Organizational Chart
4. Corporate Mission Statements and Core Values
5. Corporate Vision Statement
6. Corporate Bylaws
7. Operating Agreements
8. Shareholder Agreements
9. Capitalization Tables
10. Financial Statements and Reporting Packages
11. Operating Plans (*including Transformation Plans*)
12. Employment Agreements

Here is a list of family governance elements:

1. Family Counsel
2. Family Constitution
3. Family Mission Statements and Core Values
4. Family Vision Statement
5. Code of Conduct
6. Wills, Living Wills, and Advanced Directives
7. Philanthropic Foundation and Foundation Documents
8. Trust Documents

Once again, space constraints prevent us from going into detail on each of these vital elements, but if you would like additional information, please visit our web site for ideas, best practices, and complimentary templates.

Personal Note: *Just Say No*

I am a people pleaser. Folks tell me I am wired as a giver, not a taker.

It makes me feel good to agree with that assessment. And in fact, I proudly believe that those tendencies, along with integrity, rank among my greatest strengths as a person.

However, as often happens in life, these positive qualities can backfire and become my greatest weaknesses in certain situations. Flexibility, generosity, and naivete have served me well over the years, but they have also held me back in so many ways.

I accumulated plenty of scar tissue before I finally caught on to the fact that in order to survive and succeed, I would have to temper my people-pleasing instincts. Not all the time, and not as a first impulse, but when circumstances require.

If we meet in person someday, I bet you will think I'm a nice guy, but I'm no longer the pushover I used to be.

Now that I've made you groan by complimenting myself, I'll tell you why I brought this up.

One of the key lessons I've gleaned from life, and from business, is that you must learn how to say *"No."*

Not just no to people's requests... no to *distractions*, no to *tangents*, no to *sinkholes* that waste your time, money, volition, and emotion. No. No. No. *NO!*

I can't tell you how many times I have found myself overwhelmed by too many priorities, too many commitments, complicated relationships and dynamics that make my head spin. I become ineffective when that happens, ineffective, exhausted, and depressed.

But when my trajectory is clear, when I focus on the important things, when I shed the diversions, I move forward with strength, courage, and conviction. When I'm in that zone, you better move aside because nothing can stop me.

Clarity, simplicity, priorities, principles, and values. Cultivate them. *Insist* upon them. Protect them, and they will set you free.

That goes for your family as well, and for your business.

FOOD FOR THOUGHT EXERCISE – *LASER BEAMS*

Time to make three more lists.

List #1: T-Goals
This is hard.

The "T" in "T-Goals" stands for stands for *Tremendous* and *Target*.

If your business could only achieve one, two, or at most, three things this year, what would you want them to be? Focus hard, get specific, and *commit*.

By the way, two goals are better than three, and one is better than two. Think *laser beam*.

We don't have enough room to do this topic justice; we would need a whole book for that. Just work it. Do the best you can. You will want to bring other folks into the conversation, because if you try to do this by yourself, you will likely come up with a sub-optimal solution set.

This exercise could prove to be the most important thing you do all year.

List #2: D-Goals
Once you're clear about your T-Goals, break them down into D-Goals. 'D' stands for *Department*, *Direct*, and *Disciplined*.

Each of your departments will have their own set of D-Goals, which will guide their priorities and focus their attention. D-Goals roll up to T-Goals. This should be a simple and powerful sequence, and if you manage it right, it will turbocharge your team.

Engage each department from the beginning so you can achieve buy-in and establish the communication you will need. Work with each group to break high-level goals into sub tasks. Assign them to individuals and specify completion dates for every one.

List #3: P-Goals

'P' stands for *Personal*, *Practical*, and *Purposeful*. What do you think would happen if you defined and then achieved one to three key goals for *yourself* over the next twelve months?

I'll tell you what would happen… *Magic* would happen.

CHAPTER 12

The Principles of Scalability

O kay, now we've come to the fun stuff. This is where the mindsets and building blocks all come together. It's time to focus upon your Growth Engine, to begin scaling your business to new heights.

What do you think would be required to double the size of your business? How *long* would it take? How much would it *cost*? What steps are required to get you there? Do you even want to *try*?

What if we tripled it? This is not theoretical; people accomplish this all the time. *You can too.*

We will begin our discussion of *scalability* with a strong assertion:

> *The natural condition of a well-tuned, properly structured company is to grow.*

We presented logic behind this in an earlier summary, but it bears repeating:

> If your business provides genuine value to a well-defined set of customers,
>
> if your leadership and culture are effective and positive,
>
> if your business model holds water and can generate sustainable cash flow,
>
> if you have a capable and well-aligned team of people,
>
> if your people are backed by solid facilities, equipment, and technology, and
>
> if they execute measurable, repeatable, and productive work processes…
>
> … then your company will *grow*. That is the essence of *scalability*.

Genuine value, positive culture, profitable economics, capable people, solid infrastructure, and effective processes. *How can you argue with that?*

If you keep those six key elements dialed into your business, the only things that can hold you back will be change, competition, and capital. These are by no means trivial, but they *are* surmountable. The only other necessary ingredient is transformation. If you build that in too, then the sky is the limit.

In the next chapter, we will dig into specific implementation details. But first, let's look at some of the fundamental principles you need to embrace in order to make scalability happen.

Natural Growth Systems

Many examples of scalability exist in the natural world. We call them natural growth systems, and it helps to internalize the idea before you think about growing your business. Here are a few examples:

Trees. Consider the humble acorn, the pit of your next avocado, or one of those propeller-looking pods that spin down from maple trees. If you take those seeds, plant them in proper soil, or in the case of the avocado, suspend it in a glass of water from a few toothpicks, the seeds will sprout. Then, if you provide the proper temperature, a few sprinkles of water, appropriate sunlight, and perhaps a bit of fertilizer, they will grow. They will transform from little woody bits, to fragile seedlings, to hearty saplings, and finally to mature, seed-bearing forty-footers.

Unless you physically chop them down, or remove one or more of the proper conditions, you cannot stop this process. Their natural state is to grow.

Babies. If you feed her, give her plenty of hugs, keep her clean and safe, let her sleep when she wants, and change her diaper occasionally, she will grow. You cannot stop her, and if you're like me, it will seem that she grows way too fast.

Airplanes. This is a slightly different example, but we love it, because it reflects one of the first companies in our entrepreneurial portfolio. It was an ultralight airplane factory called SR-1 Aviation, way back in 1984. A properly trimmed airplane will fly. That is its natural state. Take a plane like that to the end of the runway, set its flaps into proper position, turn it into the wind, and open the throttle; you won't be able to hold it on the ground. It will go up, just like your sales and profits will increase if you design scalability into your company.

We apologize if this feels pedantic. The point may seem obvious on the surface, but it's worth emphasizing, because if you look at your company through the lens of natural growth, you will begin to see it in a different light.

> You will instinctively understand that the challenge is not to force growth, but to *unlock* it.

Your Money Machine

Hillary Hahn is a *music* machine. She makes it seem so easy, and she makes us cry with her phrasing and her tone. When Hillary plays her violin, you know she's working. You can see the intensity, almost feel the strength humming from her arms into her bow and the fingerboard of her instrument, which was produced by Jean-Baptiste Vuillaume in 1864. Of course, she's working hard, but her motions are so fluid and graceful, and the resulting sounds are so effortless, she seems to float above the earthly bounds of our mortal world.

You could say the same for Serena Williams' serve, Tiger Woods' swing, and Steph Curry's jump shot. Tremendous power, precision, nuance, and strength. But they make it flow so easily somehow, don't they? So natural and full of grace.

Well, as we're sure you know, that effortlessness is an illusion. Imagine the thousands, perhaps tens or hundreds of thousands of hours serious artists spend learning the basics, absorbing advice, practicing the fundamentals, achieving speed and endurance through exercise and repetition.

Hyper commitment, and attention to detail, core values, and high standards, enables them to achieve *unconscious competency*, which in turn, allows them to focus their higher faculties upon the subtle nuances that lead to sublime beauty and winning.

These people also enjoy the benefits of proper structure. Their practice routines are consistent and carefully orchestrated. Their synapses fire faster than ours do. They are the perfect height, with shoulders just wide enough, and quicker fast-twitch muscles, whatever *that* means.

The metaphor extends directly to companies. As with musicians and athletes, if you incorporate proper structure, identify and hammer on the basics, and then work the system, harder and smarter than other companies in your space, you will succeed, and your company will grow.

Do that, and you will have a successful money machine. Effort goes in at the top, and money comes out the bottom.

Perhaps we shouldn't have used superstars as examples, because we may have given you the wrong impression. You don't have to be a once-in-a-century phenomenon to have a successful money machine. You don't have to be Apple, or Google, or Ferrari to succeed across multiple generations. You simply must provide consistent, solid value to a clearly defined group of customers, repeatedly, learning as you go, gaining momentum and strength as time goes on.

When it comes to scalability, structure counts, so do high standards and practice, constant adaptation and fine tuning. You can do this. *You can build a scalable money machine.*

10x Your Business By Thinking Inside the Box

As a business owner or CEO, arguably your most important job is to develop your company's capacity to grow. And then, of course, you and your team need to execute.

As we discussed above, a blind push to sell more probably won't work. Forced growth is undependable, expensive, and risky in multiple ways. We all know companies that have imploded during periods of hyper expansion, and history is full of businesses that petered out due to lack of forward motion.

The best way to avoid these traps is to pursue scalability, to purposefully cultivate *controlled expansion* that can sustain consistent positive outcomes. Scalability is strategic and deliberate, proactive and process driven. It is safer than forced growth. Over the long term, scaling is manageable, and it enhances the value of your business.

It also helps to have a simple organizing principle, and for us it's all about the box.

Companies normally don't grow in linear fashion like an inflating balloon. Rather, they progress in steps, from one box to another, bigger boxes each time, filling them in turn, with similar but ever-evolving constraints within each.

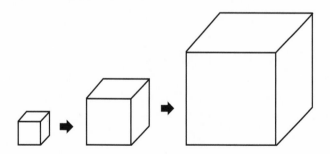

We have a name for this; we call it 10x. It's not what you might think at first. We're not talking about making your company 10 times bigger, although eventually, you probably will. Rather, 10x is a methodology for evolving from one set of constraints to the next, while enhancing the profitability of your company at each stage. Here's how it works.

A box has three dimensions: height, width, and depth. When you multiply the lengths of the three dimensions together, you calculate the volume of the box.

It is helpful to think about your company's box in similar terms: Height corresponds to *revenue*. Width corresponds to *profit*. Depth corresponds to *customer value*. We call the volume of your company's box its *stakeholder impact*.

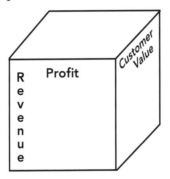

When you double the sides of a box, you cube its volume. 2 x 2 x 2 = 8.

In similar fashion, when you double your company's revenue, profit, and customer value, you will achieve 8x growth in your *stakeholder impact*.

If you enhance the profitability and quality of your offerings, just a little bit, along the way, you can drive your improvement from 8x to 10x. That's the logic behind 10x.

Your job, as a leader in your company, is to be working on the next box while your company is expanding to the edges of its current box.

This is important. You need to stay ahead of the game, because if you wait until your company bumps up against the edges of its current box without having the next one ready, it will impede your progress, and it will cost you far more to transition to the next box than it would have if you had laid proper groundwork ahead of time.

Michael Gerber, in his wonderful book, *The EMyth Revisited*, coined a phase we use every day:

> "Work *on* your company, not just *in* your company."

We mentioned a client company called Dakota Teen Triumph in the last chapter. Let's look at that excellent operation. They are building scalability into their organization as we speak, and it is transforming the business.

Scalability At Dakota Teen Triumph

DTT is owned by four siblings, two sisters and two brothers. They started it together a few years ago, and all four of them work in the business; some are fulltime, and some contribute on a part-time basis.

The company emerged from tragic circumstances, sparked by the death of a wonderful young woman, the daughter of one of the founders. At that point, all the siblings knew for sure is that they wanted to help other teens and their families thrive, protect themselves from trauma, and help them cope when life becomes too difficult to endure on their own.

The founders are all caring and intelligent, with high integrity and individual expertise. Some of them have graduate degrees, and all of them came to the challenge backed by plenty of real-world experience. However, until they launched the company, none of the siblings had ever worked in the behavioral health industry. This was brand new territory; none of the sisters or brothers were therapists or formally trained to treat troubled teens, but that didn't stop them for a minute.

Somehow, they just knew they could find a better way. They jumped in with all eight feet, investing their money, their time, and their passion. Three years later, when we got involved, they had already built out a beautiful facility, recruited a solid team of twenty-five people, and transformed the lives of hundreds of clients.

Dakota Teen Triumph originally retained us to help clarify and structure the family side of their ownership challenge. They weren't experiencing severe difficulty, but they could see that as time goes on, especially when second-generation cousins become involved in the business, they are going to need additional structure and clear ground rules in order to stay in harmony and on track.

We started with a weekend retreat, where we worked hard to articulate the mission and core values of the organization. Then we turned our attention to corporate governance, creating a plan to upgrade and formalize the board of directors. All four of the siblings are on the board, so structure and formality are essential in order to prevent board meetings from devolving into casual family reunions.

Speaking of family, the siblings also created an owner's council, which enables them to meet periodically and focus directly upon family dynamics and communication.

Once the basic governance elements were in place, we turned our attention to the business itself. We started by transforming the leadership team from a group of committed and highly engaged individual players, who primarily supported the CEO, into a tightly integrated group of leaders who consistently drive results through their departmental teams. We accomplished this through training and stretching, not replacement. Most of the senior leaders are still with the company.

In addition to training, we introduced and developed T-Goals, D-Goals, and performance metrics that the leadership team uses to guide its priorities and efforts. These goals are clear, and everyone in the organization knows what they are. This keeps all the stakeholders on the same page, enabling everyone to understand where we are today and where we intend to be tomorrow.

An important early part of this process involved upgrading the accounting, finance, and budgeting infrastructure, with clarity and scalability as our top objectives. We transitioned from cash to accrual accounting, built a small and effective initial team, formalized financial controls, implemented clear, consistent reporting, and created a new forecasting model, with departmental budgets, that would enable the board and the leadership team to understand their status and manage their forward progress.

Each of the operating groups—clinical, program, admissions, billing, and outreach—executed a similar process. We developed a scalable organizational structure, unpacked specific individuals who were stressed from trying to do too many things, and crystalized each of the underlying departmental teams, placing heavy emphasis upon empathy, accountability, and trust.

Dakota Teen Triumph is still a work in progress. It will always be so, but it is now far more scalable, and the owners are turning their attention to expanding the reach of the organization, through increasing the capacity of their initial facility and by opening additional centers, throughout the local region and beyond.

This isn't rocket science, but it is highly satisfying work, especially since the underlying mission contributes so many priceless gifts to the world. We are grateful to have the opportunity to collaborate with the owners of Dakota Teen Triumph, and we are serious about our commitment to the behavioral health industry. This is truly good work, and we feel exceedingly fortunate.

A Personal Note: *Pushing the Rope Uphill*

When I was a kid, my father introduced me to the concept of pushing the rope uphill. He used that phrase frequently, and I've found it to be a useful metaphor, in so many ways, ever since.

It's easy to pull a rope, but it's pretty darn hard to *push* one. Pushing a rope, especially uphill, goes against the natural order of things; the rope bunches up, and leaves you sitting there stuck.

So many sales managers and business books espouse a rope-pushing approach. They come across as aggressive, forceful, sometimes even manipulative, and they always leave me cold. They encourage us to attack our challenges by shoving on that poor old rope, pushing the darn thing up the hill, when instead, they should be showing us how to unlock natural growth and progress.

I used to approach sales that way. I used to think the key was to *sell harder*, to make more cold calls, memorize closing techniques, radiate confidence, deliver more donuts, get my courage up, and then stress out because I couldn't think of what else I needed to do.

Now I know that it's about *attraction*, not force. Gently reeling in the rope, never pushing it. Earning that attraction through value, high quality, and attention to detail, by humbly solving problems and satisfying genuine needs, serving people who trust your company because it delivers the goods, every time at a fair price.

That's how you achieve scalability. Build a money machine and incorporate the elements we described above. Then work on that machine, constantly tinkering, striving for improvement, recognizing and even anticipating the needs and desires of your tribe of customers and other stakeholders. That way, you will stay on top of your game and ahead of your competition. That is how you unlock natural growth and keep it flowing over time.

My father, Gerald K. Fisher, died three years ago. He taught me so many things. I miss him every day.

FOOD FOR THOUGHT EXERCISE– *THE RULE OF SEVENTY-TWO*

This isn't a scalability factor, but it's a fun and useful tool, a mathematical rule of thumb you can use to plan and measure your progress.

It's simple: *Divide seventy-two by an annual sales growth rate, and the result will tell you approximately how many years it will take to double the size of your company.*

Here are some examples:

5 percent annual growth $72 \div 5 = 14.4$ years to double your company

10 percent annual growth $72 \div 10 = 7.2$ years to double your company

13 percent annual growth $72 \div 13 = 5.5$ years to double your company

Of course, since this is simple math, it's easy to switch things around and answer a different question:

Roughly, what annual growth rate would we need to achieve in order to double the size of our company in X number of years?

Double in eight years $72 \div 8 = 9$ 9 percent annual growth rate to double in eight years

Double in six years $72 \div 6 = 12$ 12 percent annual growth rate to double in six years

Double in four years $72 \div 4 = 18$ 18 percent annual growth rate to double in four years

Play around with this a bit. Get a feeling for the underlying relationships. Compare them to your experience, then decide how soon you want to double the size of your business.

We *know* you can make it happen, and we are here to help you.

CHAPTER 13

Implementing Scalability

Business owners and leadership teams often turn their attention to *scalability* when they are worried about one of two existential problems:

They feel stuck. They know they could be growing faster. They want to understand what's holding them back, and they want to strengthen the engagement of their family and accelerate the growth of their business.

They want their growth to be safer and more sustainable. They worry that uncontrolled growth might lead to quality problems and reduced profitability, so they want to reduce risk, make their operations more predictable, and streamline day-to-day management.

In order to address these challenges, we created the *Family Business Management System*. All the elements we have explored in this book culminate here, so you can safely build scalability into your company. There is no guarantee that you will succeed, but *scalability* will increase your chances, and it will enhance your peace of mind by orders of magnitude.

As mentioned before, the management system organizes the elements of your company into *six scalabilities,* six areas of focus, which underpin your organization. Dial these in, pay attention to each one, track and adapt them as time goes on, and you will unlock healthy and manageable natural growth.

Here are the six scalabilities:

1. *Leadership and Culture*

2. *Market Focus and Fit*

3. *Business Model and Finance*

4. *Team Alignment and Capacity*

5. *Infrastructure and Technology*

6. *Systems and Work Processes*

The appendix presents a list of food-for-thought questions related to each one.

The next book in our *Family Business Abundance Series* will address scalability in greater detail.

We look forward to working from that larger canvas, and we feel slightly frustrated that the overview nature of *this* book forces us to address the Scalabilities from a high altitude, but please, *do* give it a go. The scalabilities will change your life, if you invite them in.

SCALABILITY #1: Leadership And Culture

It all starts here. Your first job is to ensure that you have the culture, leadership, decision-making, and governance required to stabilize your business, and to enable your team to follow the path to fruition.

Bedrock Elements of Culture

Mission. A strong, compelling mission, that explains the *purpose* of your company, *why* it exists.

Core Values. Decisive core values, incontrovertible and non-negotiable, describing what you *stand* for.

Vision. Clearly defined vision, specific, big, and compelling enough to *bind* your people together.

Priorities. Transparent priorities expressed as company goals that roll down into each department.

These elements will fuel a cohesive culture, accountable and resilient enough to respond to external threats and adapt to changing market conditions.

You need to be explicit about these elements. Create them together with your family and your team; don't impose them after dreaming them up on your own. That way, people will be more likely to buy in and commit.

Be consistent. Communicate the elements clearly and often, every chance you get, across any media that comes your way. Live up to your culture every day. Make sure everyone understands, remembers, and buys into each piece.

Leadership Team

You don't want a bunch of yes-men and yes-women jumping at your every whim. That might feel good for some people, but you cannot scale your company that way. You must cultivate a team of professionals who can ensure that the work gets done, while helping you understand where you are all at all times, a team of professionals who can truly *lead* their departments, while supporting one another, constantly tracking progress, and driving ongoing improvement into every area of your business.

Consider the words leadership and team. Stop for a moment and think about what those words mean; they say it all. These are not *yes-people*, and they are not just individual players. They truly are, and must be, the team that will lead your company forward. After the bedrock cultural elements, developing and supporting this team should be your single, most important priority.

The last thing we will emphasize about this infinitely important issue of the leadership team, is how crucial it is to foster trust and healthy conflict. That means you need to cultivate unconditional support for one another, and the free exchange of ideas and opinions. Please beware. It is easy to convince yourself that just because you are meeting with your department heads and bringing them into the discussion, that you are creating a truly functional leadership team. It will take the members a while to believe you. At first, they are likely to nod their heads, express agreement with your pronouncements, and keep right on letting that monkey cling to *your* back.

Leadership team development is often the top priority during the initial stages of our engagements with client families and companies. Get help or do it yourself, but no matter what, please take the time and effort to build a *truly* functional leadership team. Then support and nurture them while they *run* the company for you.

Decision Making

Most people crave structure and predictability. In order to focus upon their work, these folks need to be comfortable, which means they need to understand the consequences of their actions and how decisions get made within the organization.

Think about your style and how it impacts decision-making across your departments. There is no right answer here, but clarity and consistency are essential. Are you inclined toward command-and-control? Consensus? Enlightened dictatorship?

What is the chain of command? How stable is it, and how transparent?

We advocate a style that involves leadership team consensus, governed by a CEO who makes firm calls in the rare event that the group is divided. Most of the time, your leadership team will know what the right decision is. If you have buy-in, supported by the free exchange of ideas and opinions, your decisions will be more likely to be right, they will be more likely to stick, and people will execute them with a higher degree of confidence.

Strategic Governance

You need a board of directors, and it must be functional (as opposed to *dysfunctional*), which means that it needs to be well-informed, apolitical, somewhat independent, and willing to put the best interests of the company and its mission above all else.

In most companies, especially family businesses, this means that you should include one or more independent board members who are not owners or part of the family. The job of the board is to hire, evaluate, and fire the CEO, and to guide the management team on strategic issues. With very rare exception, the board should *not* be involved in day-to-day operations or operational decisions.

SCALABILITY #2: Market Focus And Fit

This is an area where the concept of pushing a rope uphill really comes into play, and it's a trap we must avoid at all costs. We must be clear and thoughtful about what we are selling, and to whom we are selling. We must make sure we have well-defined, attractive markets, with clear opportunities to deliver value to addressable customers, a strong strategic foundation, and plenty of room to grow.

Foundation

We begin with the most fundamental questions:

Mission. What is the mission of our company? What changes do we aim to make in the world?

Core Values. What are the core values that guide our efforts and our decisions?

Core Competencies. What are we truly good at, the core competencies that will differentiate us?

Core Customers. Who are our core customers, the people and organizations we choose to serve?

Core Offerings. Based upon these elements, what are our core offerings, the products and services we will focus upon most intensely?

The foundation elements come first because they provide the bedrock upon which we build our company. These will evolve over time, but carefully, with deliberate intention, and supported by data.

Markets And Tribe

Once we are clear about why we are in business, what we stand for, what we are best at, who we aim to serve, and how we intend to serve them, we proceed to the next level.

We develop a deep understanding of what motivates our customers and the referral sources who help us spread the word. This is our tribe, and we must know what makes them tick. Here are a few questions that can help you get there:

1. What do our customers and referral sources really want from us?

2. What jobs are they hiring us to do?

3. What are their pain points, and how intense is that pain?

4. How urgent are each of their needs? (*When are we selling aspirin, and when are we selling vitamins?*)

5. Do we have a robust product/market fit here, or is this a temporary anomaly?

6. Is our relationship with our customer meaningful?

7. Are we delivering enough true value to enable us to grow and sustain profitable operations going forward?

We need to be especially clear about our primary markets, and our key customer segments. We build them from the ground up, and we must understand how fast they are growing. It's much easier to expand from within a tide that raises all boats, rather than fighting the currents of declining markets. The metaphor of a melting ice cube presents a depressing image, but it is a helpful one when it comes to avoiding difficult markets and customer segments.

We also need to know which other companies and substitutes are competing for our customers and our markets. That means today *and* tomorrow. We need to know how strong they are, how they position themselves, and how easy it will be to differentiate ourselves and grab market share from their clutches.

Customer Experience

It's necessary, but not enough, to know who our customers are and what provides their motivation. We must also walk many miles in their moccasins. We must understand, at a deep level, what our tribe members experience when they engage with us.

Then we must constantly fine-tune that experience along many dimensions, so they remain delighted by our interactions, so it's easy to work with us, and so the benefits that come from our offerings exceed their expectations in memorable ways.

This is how we begin to unlock natural growth. It's a huge undertaking, but it is essential, and well worth the effort. Here are some questions you should ask yourself at this stage:

1. What do people want to feel when they interact with our brand? Are they looking for smart? For sporty? For high-fashion, or bawdy humor?

2. What colors will best reflect our customers' desires? How should that affect our design sensibilities, and how should we modulate the tone of our '*voice*'?

3. What can we do to ensure that our web site, ads, and other communications consistently reflect the experience our Tribe is looking for?

4. Do each of the underlying processes that comprise our customer experience—attraction, information gathering, exploration, initial decision, purchase, delivery, customer support, and repeat engagement—seamlessly lead from one to the next, satisfying people every step of the way?

5. What can we do to make it easier, safer, more pleasant, and more rewarding to work with us, and to refer us to other customers?

Brand Elements

Once we understand the fundamental requirements of our customer experience, we generate our brand elements, the names, colors, logos, templates, and communication guidelines that will most likely evoke the feelings and value that our tribe members seek.

The levels of this pyramid are sequential, to some degree. You need to do your best to optimize each level before proceeding to the next. But this is also an iterative process, and it is never-ending. Over time, you should move back and forth, up and down the pyramid, to make sure that you remain vital and dialed in as your Tribe and your markets evolve.

Lead Generation And Outreach

If you've laid proper groundwork at prior levels, it will be much easier, less expensive, and less mysterious to identify and attract people who are interested in what you have to offer. Lead generation is not free, but it is a natural process that will almost drive itself if you have the proper foundation, targeting, experience, and brand elements in place.

Once you have nailed the fundamentals, you can implement plans and processes that enable you to reach out to the people who want what you have. Yes, this is *selling*, online, in the field, and on the ground.

You can plan your activities and your spending, and you can measure the outcomes of this work, constantly comparing results across campaigns and promotions, tweaking your approach and testing new ideas, all the while, ensuring that you deliver on your promise to your customers with consistent care and attention.

Here is a diagram of the marketing topic pyramid we just reviewed.

SCALABILITY #3: Business Model And Finance

This is the bottom line, of course. At least, this is what most people mean when they evoke the phrase "bottom line". But we wonder why, if it's so important, do so few business owners and executives invest enough time and resources to truly understand the financial aspects of their operations?

Financial Drivers

Every money machine has a set of knobs that can track and help influence the performance of the machine. We need to know these knobs, inside and out. Each person on the leadership team, including and especially you, needs to be comfortable and fluent in the language of your company's financial drivers.

We need to uncover, analyze, and optimize the mechanics of the company's cash flow, how it *makes money*. We need to understand both the big picture and the low-level unit economics of each one of our key transactions.

This will enable us to estimate the sustainability of our business model, along with the primary threats that could derail it. To do that, we need to be clear about the key costs and variables that determine the profitability of our transactions and other activities. For example, on average:

Acquisition Cost. What does it cost for us to acquire each customer?

Lifetime Value. How much will each customer spend on our offerings over time?

Gross Margin. How much does it cost for us to make and/or deliver our products and services, before marketing and overhead expenses?

Price Elasticity. How does customer demand for our offerings change as our prices go up and down?

Breakeven. How many units do we need to sell in order to begin making money?

Cost Containment. Where are the opportunities for us to reduce our costs without compromising quality?

The list goes on, and the details are important. If you and your Leadership Team approach it right, this can become a fun process, a big game with satisfaction and money in the end for everyone.

Status and Performance Reporting

In addition to the financial drivers of our business, we need to understand exactly where we are today, no rose-colored glasses. As best we can, we also need to understand where we *want* to go, and where we're headed now. We need to understand what resources we have at our disposal, and we need to have contingency plans to protect us when we make unexpected mistakes, or our predictions of the future are too far off base.

Once you understand your drivers, you will be able to create metrics, a simple reflection of your drivers, that you can incorporate into your reporting and track over time. Good metrics are the key to success. If you can't measure it, you can't manage it, and if you can't manage it, well, you're in trouble…

To make all this work, we need consistent, regular, simple, and accurate reporting. It needs to arrive on time, some of it weekly, some of it monthly. We need to digest these reports in our leadership team meetings. We need to understand them, poke them full of holes, and leverage them to improve our performance.

If you put solid reporting in place and take the time to really use it, your blood pressure will drop, and your dreams will be sweeter.

Financial Controls, Capital Base, And Strategy

If we had more space, we would dig deeply into each of these areas. They are all vital to the wellbeing of your financial operation, however, so we encourage you to review and consider the questions in the appendix, and please be sure to reach out or visit our website if you would like additional materials or guidance.

SCALABILITY #4: Team Alignment And Capacity

Once we're clear about our culture, our markets, and our money, we need to direct our attention to our *people*. We need to understand how cohesive the team is, how tightly each person aligns with our mission, core values, vision, and priorities. We need to be clear about how our departments are organized, and how effective the structures are, relative to our mission and our plans. Long term, alignment is priceless and crucial. It will help keep us strong, resilient, and well positioned to adapt over time.

Once we're aligned around alignment, we need to evaluate the capacity of each underlying team, leader, and individual contributor. If it's properly designed, our organizational chart will help us immeasurably.

It is difficult to achieve true objectivity in this area, but we must do our best. It helps to lean on our mission, core values, and standards. They provide a useful gauge you can use to estimate and measure the motivation, capacities, and needs of every team member. We must develop our team so we can be proud of each person. Everyone should have their place, and every individual and department should be fully accountable.

If you establish and manage your leadership team in proper fashion, these ongoing tasks will become much easier. Organizational growth will become more natural as the leadership team extends its influence into your departmental teams. It will be obvious when someone doesn't fit in, and it will be much easier, and better for everyone, to disengage from the people who aren't actively bailing water out of your lifeboat.

SCALABILITY #5: Infrastructure And Technology

Remember when we discussed thinking inside the box in the last chapter? Well, the box is the star of the show here.

In addition to the market, financial, and HR dynamics discussed above, we need to understand the other constraints we're operating under, including physical, technical, compliance, legal and other aspects. If our current box is too restrictive, we need to construct a bigger one before we can scale. And as soon as we get that one in place, of course, we need to begin thinking about the next one.

Infrastructure is such an interesting word. Infrastructure can be defined as this:

The basic physical and organizational structures and facilities (e.g. buildings, roads, power supplies) needed for the operation of a society or enterprise.

Physical facilities are obvious. They include your office space, furniture, factory floors, vehicles, production machinery, computers and other hardware, etc. Our treatment of physical infrastructure will be brief, but there are two points worth emphasizing:

Plan your moves well in advance and act early. If you wait until you actually need the extra space or equipment, you're too late, because transitions always take longer than you think, opportunity costs are high when you're constrained by physical realities, and perhaps most important, you lose much of your negotiating leverage if you wait until you're desperate.

Carefully analyze and consider the long-term implications of your physical infrastructure. Lease terms are obvious examples of this, and of course, you need to carefully account for them. You also need to be keenly aware of production-related capacity constraints, future expense commitments, load balancing, maintenance costs, return on capital, and other dynamics related to your hard assets.

What about the organizational structures? Well, we find it helpful to lay out three categories of non-physical infrastructure:

1. Legal and compliance

2. Finance

3. Technology and data management

Legal And Compliance

An important aspect of your legal infrastructure involves your corporate documents, including LLC agreements or articles of incorporation, shareholder agreements, bylaws, capitalization tables, and various other documents that define your business, lay out the ground rules, and specify who owns what. You need to have these in place, and we recommend that you understand them personally. Find good legal counsel that can help you with this. If you wait until you are in trouble or have a dispute, you will regret it.

The next layer of legal infrastructure involves compliance, which includes state licensing, required record keeping, industry-specific inspections and accreditation, and tax matters, among other things. Again, we recommend that you lean on strong legal counsel whom you can trust. These issues can seriously come back to bite you if you're not careful.

The third level of legal infrastructure involves contracts and agreements, and the fourth, raising its ugly head, involves litigation and dispute resolution. Depending upon the size and complexity of your operation, you may want to develop a combination of in-house and external counsel that can keep you on a safe and easy track. We recommend that you take all commitments, agreements, and requirements seriously, and be sure to keep your leadership team members informed and at least somewhat involved in all important deliberations and negotiations.

Finance

Finance has its own scalability, of course, and we already discussed various elements of it. However, we find it useful to consider the structural elements of your finance operations in the infrastructure camp as well. It helps in the long run if you consciously construct your financial controls, reporting packages, transaction procedures, and other elements as if they are physically manifested. Make them strong, as bulletproof as you can. You will be glad you did.

Technology And Data Management

This infrastructure type rhymes with the finance category. Your hardware is part of your physical infrastructure, computers, servers, mobile devices, phone systems, video screens, cameras, etc. But the way you *manage* your technology equipment, the way you research, acquire, deploy, track, protect, and repair it, represents an important infrastructure category.

In today's world, data is arguably one of the most valuable assets your company owns, and the more you manage it, the more valuable it becomes. Data is not physical, but you need to treat it as if it is. This deserves your attention, along with significant investments in money, time, creativity, security, and communication.

As usual, space doesn't permit a full treatment of each infrastructure area, but they are all crucial, and if improperly addressed, any one of them can impose deal-killer constraints that impede your progress from one box to the next.

SCALABILITY #6: Systems and Work Processes

Finally, once you have addressed the other dimensions of your business, it is time to focus upon the operational processes that make everything happen. Until you understand the other scalabilities, it doesn't make sense to spend too much time in this area, but once you get here, few factors are more important to the well-being and performance of your organization.

Work processes permeate every aspect of your company. There are tons of overlap here between this scalability and the other five. Each scalability and infrastructure item depends upon well-crafted and managed work processes for its survival.

If your company is a money machine, then your work processes are the pistons, gears, fuel lines, and transmission that will determine your scalability and generate forward motion.

One of the most difficult, and fun, aspects of business building involves designing, monitoring, and optimizing the work processes required to produce your offerings and distribute them to your clients. And the processes are by no means only product related. Think about the finance processes we described above, and what about HR, legal, compliance, technology, and data management? The list goes on and on, and each process that appears on that list represents an opportunity to delight your customer just a bit more, make a little more money, strengthen alignment with your team members, sharpen your focus, and make better decisions.

Your company is a money machine, and you are the lead engineer. We repeat: Work *on* your business, not just *in* your business.

A Personal Note: *From Friend, To Boss, To Leader*

If you want to build scalability into your company, the first thing you must transform is *you*.

It doesn't matter what generation you're in or which role you occupy; you need to build scalability into *yourself*. You must change... increase your knowledge, hone your skills, and expand your perspective. Evolve as a *leader*.

I like to think that *I'm* a great leader. In my imagination, that's certainly the case. I also happen to be six feet tall in my mind's eye. In the real world, *not so much* (five feet, seven inches). But one thing I can say for sure: *I am a better leader than I used to be*.

I have worked hard on leadership over the years. I've read books, taken classes, attended speeches, endured 360 evaluations, paid for coaching, and tried my best to manage hundreds of people across more than three decades. It's a never-ending process, but I'm glad I'm in the game.

Before you read on, stop to consider the following outline. See if it makes sense; I'll explain below. The outline highlights key insights I gained as I tried to evolve from a naïve, young entrepreneur into what I hope is a more effective leader.

a. Friend ➜ Boss

b. Boss ➜ Leader

c. Answers ➜ Questions

d. Reactive ➜ Proactive

e. Instincts ➜ Metrics

f. "Calls" and Decisions ➜ Vision, Principles, Plans, and Process

g. Hero ➜ Facilitator and Teacher

h. Order Giver ➜ Credit Giver and Blame Taker

i. Visionary CEO ➜ Nurturing Guide

j. Personal Gain ➜ Mission

k. Manage Everybody ➜ Empower the Executive Team

At the beginning, I wanted to be everyone's friend. But after much frustration and lackluster performance (mostly on *my* part), I concluded that I needed to be the *boss*, to tell everyone what to *do*. So, I went through a control phase, but that just made everyone miserable, including me. Gradually, I learned that the role of the CEO, and this goes for owners too, is to *lead* the company, not '*run*' it. That insight made a big difference for me.

After that, I learned about questions. I had previously assumed that as CEO, my job was to have all the answers. I'm the boss, right? I need to know what's going on, call the shots. Well, after a few years of this ridiculousness, it finally dawned on me that my job was to ask the *questions*, not have the answers. And to ask the questions with genuine curiosity, with an open mindset that encourages people to think for themselves. Then to listen to the answers; really listen.

Here's another lesson for which I am grateful: Stop being so *reactive* all the time. Strong instincts are priceless, but don't allow them to rule your life, like some gunslinger from the Old West. Factor your instincts in but find some distance and think things through, back your reactions up with data and metrics. As Ronald Reagan said: "Trust but verify."

The leader's job is not to make the calls and decisions, at least not often. The leader's job is to help define the vision, reinforce key principles, identify objectives, formulate plans, and refine processes. Please notice that I used the word *"help"* in the last sentence. The leader doesn't dictate. She provides guidance, helps the team conceptualize and then adhere to those crucial drivers.

I went through a phase when I thought my job was to *delegate*, to give *orders*. I was the hero of the movie. But after struggling for a few years, I concluded that I'm *not* the hero. My role is to be a guide, a coach, a developer of capable people.

I learned that rather than giving orders and calling shots, it is better to give credit to others for the good things, and to accept blame for the bad. This is hard, and it can hurt, but that's what people need. It's fine to be a visionary CEO, but in my book, it's even better to nurture the talent, capacity, and vision of others. By the way, that doesn't mean that you don't establish boundaries, clear expectations, and accountability. Of course, you foster those disciplines. But you need to create systems and capacities that bring the disciplines to life, so you don't have to run around yelling all the time.

It is clear to me now that the leadership challenge is not about personal gain or glory. It is about the *Mission*. Why are we doing this? Why are we here together? What is our *purpose*? Those are the questions you need to ask and help answer. You're not there to manage everything; you are there to empower your people, especially your leadership team.

There is a reason that *Leadership and Culture* is the first Scalability in our Family Business Management System. When we work with business owners, we *always* start there. That's how you drive the best and most lasting transformations. And the first thing you must transform is *you*.

FOOD FOR THOUGHT EXERCISE – YOUR BUSINESS LIBRARY

Some of the greatest gifts I have received have come from the books I've read. They have, um, *literally* transformed my life, many times over. If you've gotten this far in the book, I'm guessing that you're a reader too. It's nice to share pages with a kindred spirit.

You probably have a collection of wonderful books in your past, just as I do. That's good, because if you are going to be scalable as a person, you must continue to cram your cranium full of new knowledge and ideas, along multiple dimensions.

I encourage you to put together your own collection. Find a quiet moment. Shut your eyes or grab a piece of paper, then force yourself to remember and acknowledge some of the key books you've read in recent years. What did you learn from each? Why did you like it so much? What changes did you make as a result? With whom did you share it?

CHAPTER 14

Conclusion

A n adage says: You can never be too rich or too thin. *We disagree.* Rich and thin don't matter in the end. Here's what it should be:

> You can never be too engaged, too clear, or too scalable.

With that in mind, here is a final recap of the main points asserted by the *Family Business Management System:*

Family Business Abundance is an excellent and worthy goal. It is the most effective way to build multi-generational wealth, and the benefits are well worth striving for.

Our enterprise is a *Family Business*, not just a family-owned business. There is a big difference.

A *Family Business Growth Engine* will sustain our family for the next 100 years. Passive portfolios are wonderful, but they won't cut it alone. We need to develop the power to create new wealth.

We will work hard to cultivate *engagement* that will bring our family members together and connect them to our business.

We will strive to bring *clarity* to our business and to our family, to illuminate all the dark corners of our business and gain strength through transparency.

We will build *scalability* into our business, creating a solid structure that can enable our family to thrive and expand for the next 100 years or more.

Where Will Your Family And Your Business Be In 100 Years?

No one knows for sure, of course, but you can decide where you *want* them to be. What do you hope happens to *you*, to your *family*, and to your *business* over the coming decades and generations?

Throughout this book, we have spoken directly to *you*. That wasn't just artifice. In so many ways, it is up to you to take the initiative, for yourself and for your family.

We believe in families and in family business. We genuinely care about whether you pursue your dreams, where you end up, and how you look back after it's all said and done. That is why we are in this line of work, and that is why we wrote this book.

Perhaps we've met you already. Maybe that pleasure is yet to come, and of course, there is a chance that our paths will never cross, except between these pages.

Well, no matter. What counts is that you are here, that we are here together. We thank you for sharing part of your journey with us.

Advisors who are reading this book will likely be thinking about their clients. If you are an advisor, and if you agree with our assertions, perhaps you are wondering how you can incorporate some of these ideas into your practice. We would consider it a compliment if you did, and we would gladly help you do so. Please reach out to us if that is the case.

If you are a business owner or a family member, we hope you found concepts, tools, perspective, and encouragement that can help you muster the strength to take your family and your business to the next level. *We know you can do it.*

Your Purpose, Your Family, And Your Business

Nothing could be more important than those three gifts, except perhaps the fertile combination of thoughts and emotions swimming around in your head right now. We hope you feel just a bit more conviction, a bit more imagination, a bit more enthusiasm and resilience after our time together.

Thank you again for reading this book.

Now onward, and best of luck to you and your family. Please stay in touch. We intend to be right here with you for the next 100 years or more.

Scalability RoadMap
Discussion Outline

One of our favorite program offerings involves helping our family business clients assess the current state of their scalabilities, compare them with the details of their vision statement, and build a high-level plan that will help them get from here to there.

We call this the Scalability RoadMap, and we are happy to share the basic questions you need to draft a roadmap of your own. Please visit our website for additional complementary materials if you would like a bit more support.

Similar treatments are available for engagement and clarity, but we don't want to overwhelm you with too much detail, so we've limited ourselves here to scalability.

As you recall, we identified six scalabilities that you can harness to enhance your company's ability to grow, without compromising quality or profitability:

1. *Leadership and Culture*

2. *Market Focus and Fit*

3. *Business Model and Finance*

4. *Team Alignment and Capacity*

5. *Infrastructure and Technology*

6. *Systems and Work Processes*

The following sections provide a series of questions for each scalability:

Leadership And Culture:

1. Mission:

   a. Does our company have a clear mission today?

   b. If not, is there an opportunity to identify a worthwhile and compelling mission?

   c. Can we get the Mission Statement down to one simple sentence that our team, our board, our strategic partners, and our customers can understand and repeat?

2. Core Values:

   a. Does our company have six to ten key core values?

   b. If so, are they written down and repeatable?

   c. If not, can we create some?

   (*If we have clear core values, we can extend them into operating principles that can help guide our hiring, service offerings, and decision making as we expand the organization.*)

3. Vision and Flexibility:

    a. How clear, strong, and ambitious is our vision?

    b. How big do we want to grow, and how fast?

    c. How does the organization cope with change?

       • Historically   • Currently   • Ideally

    d. How urgent is the need to change today?

    e. How flexible is our organization?

4. Leadership Team:

    a. Who is running the company? What exactly is the hierarchy?

    b. Is there a strong leadership team of direct reports to the CEO?

    c. What are the management and decision-making processes for that team?

    d. What key characteristics and capabilities are we looking for from the CEO and the rest of the leadership team?

    e. How do we define success for every leadership team member?

       • Do we have clear, prioritized objectives and goals?

       • Do we have a set of primary success measures and metrics for each?

       • What are the most important challenges that each person will face?

5. Culture and Priorities:

    a. How important is culture to the organization today?

    b. How strong and cohesive is our culture?

    c. How clear and regular is our communication of culture?

   d. How well are staff members and clients able to articulate our mission and values?

   e. How clear and well-communicated are the organization's priorities?

   f. What are the current key priorities for our organization?

6. Transparency and Decision Making:

   a. What is the current decision-making process, and how effective is it?

   b. How transparent is the organization?

      • Historically • Currently • Ideally

   c. What formal management structures exist in the organization?

      • How effective are each of these structures?

7. Key Constituents: (*What groups contribute to, regulate, and benefit from our work?*)

   a. Customers   g. Board of Directors

   b. Investors   h. Government Officials

   c. Patrons & Donors   i. Local Community

   d. Advisory Board   j. Regulators

   e. Staff   k. Client Families

   f. Employers/Customers l. Sub-Contractors

8. Strategic Leadership and Governance:

   a. Strategic Planning:

      • Who participates in the process?

      • How strong and clear is our strategic planning process?

- Who are the audiences, and how do we report our progress?

b. Board Oversight:

- Is there a board today? If so, how strong and functional is it?

- How many board members should we have, and who should they be?

- How can we be sure we are making the best strategic decisions?

- What kind of reporting package do we create for ourselves and the board?

c. Advisory Board:

- Does an advisory board exist? If so, how strong and functional is it?

- If not, does it make sense to establish an advisory board?

- What people or types of people should we target for membership?

- How many advisory board members should there be?

- What formal priority initiatives are in place?

- What are the opportunities for quick wins?

Market Focus And Fit:

1. What market(s) are we pursuing?

   a. How large are each of our primary markets?

   b. How many target clients are there in each?

   c. What are the primary sub-segments/niches within each market?

    d. How fast are each of the markets growing, year-over-year?

2. Customers and offerings:

    a. Who, exactly, are we selling to in each market?

    b. What exactly are we selling them today?

    c. What jobs are they asking us to do?

    d. How well do we satisfy the needs and wants behind those jobs?

    e. What are their pain points, and how strong is that pain?

    f. What motivates customers to buy each of our offerings?

    g. Are there significant new offering opportunities in each market?

3. Growth:

    a. Some initial questions:

- How big is our company today?
- How big do we want to become?
- How soon do we want to get there?
- Who are our most important target clients?
- What additional services can we provide over time?
- Where can we deliver the most value and greatest impact?
- What are the greatest growth opportunities?
- What is the best way to differentiate ourselves?

    b. What does it mean for us to grow?

- Revenue
- Profits

- Number of clients
- Number of customers
- Number of employees
- Mission Impact

c. How do we accelerate and sustain that growth?

- More current offerings to existing client groups?
- New offerings to existing client groups?
- Current offerings to new client groups?
- New offerings to new client groups?

4. Does our company have a long-term strategic plan?

a. What are the key strategic objectives?

b. What are the key financial objectives?

c. What are the impact and outcome objectives?

5. What are our most pressing product/service challenges?

• Historic   • Current   • Future

6. Competition:

a. Who are our most significant competitors?

b. What are their key strengths and areas of vulnerability?

c. How are we differentiated from them? How sustainable is that differentiation?

d. What substitute products or services are competing for our customers?

e. How strong is the inclination for our customers to do nothing?

Business Model And Finance:

1. Financial Drivers:

    a. What are our primary sources of revenue? $ and percent

    b. What are our key costs? $ and percent

    c. What are our primary transactions? And for each:

    - Average LTV (Lifetime Value of Customer)?

    - Average cost to acquire a customer?

    - Unit economics?

2. Financial Performance:

    a. How satisfied are we with our financial performance?

    b. What are our scale economies and opportunities for financial improvement?

    c. What are the primary bottlenecks and financially-based growth inhibitors?

    d. How strong is our balance sheet?

    e. How well do we manage our expenses, receivables, and payables?

    f. How timely, transparent, and helpful is our reporting?

3. Controls:

    a. Do we have clear and consistent budgets, and do we manage to them?

    b. What is the financial chain of command?

    c. Who cuts the checks, and who signs them? (Hopefully, not the same person.)

    d. What financial controls are in place?

    e. How effective are the controls?

4. Capital Base:

   a. What is our status in terms of capital and long-term sustainability?

   b. How satisfied are we with that status?

   c. How adequate is our safety cushion?

   d. Are there any other important dynamics to consider?

5. Key Metrics:

   a. What metrics do we use to measure our financial performance?

   b. How effective, clear, and accurate are our metrics?

   c. What are the frequency and timeliness of our metrics?

   d. According to the metrics, what has been our historical performance?

6. Financial Strategy:

   a. Do we have a long-term financial strategy?

   b. How clear is our financial plan?

   c. How ambitious is our financial plan?

   d. What are the key threats to our cash flow and our plan?

Team Alignment And Capacity:

1. Structure:

   a. What are the primary operating groups?

   b. What are the levels of management within each group?

   c. What are the roles and primary objectives of each group?

2. Alignment:

    a. What is the degree of alignment for each group?

- With the organization's Mission and Values?
- With the underlying objectives and priorities of the group?

3. Capacity:

    a. What are the key performance metrics for each group?

    b. How strong is the performance for each group?

- Historically • Currently • Ideally

    c. How strong is the commitment of each group leader?

    d. What is the capacity of each leader relative to the group's objectives?

    e. What is the level of support and capacity of each underlying team?

    f. How effective is the decision making in each group?

    g. What is the degree of transparency within each group?

    h. How effective is training, coaching, and mentoring in each group?

    i. How easy is it to recruit high-quality team members?

Infrastructure And Technology:

1. Legal, Finance, and Compliance:

    a. Who is on our legal team, and how is it structured?

    b. How about our accountants and auditors?

    c. Are there any material past, current, or future legal or compliance issues?

    d.   Are we subject to regulatory oversight? If so, what entities are regulating us?

    e.   How compliant are we?

    f.   What licensing and accreditation do we need, and are we current with each?

2. Facilities:

    a.   How satisfied are we with our facilities?

    b.   What are the key problems?

    c.   What is the capacity for growth within our current facilities?

    d.   How effective are our facilities in terms of workflow and communication?

    e.   How secure are our facilities?

    f.   How economical are our facilities?

3. Equipment:

    a.   How satisfied are we with our equipment?

    b.   What are the key problems?

    c.   What is the capacity for growth with our current equipment?

4. Technology:

    a.   Primary systems and applications:

- What are they?
- How effective are they?
- How secure are they?
- How cost-efficient are they?

- Do we develop our own applications? If so, who and how?

b. IT Management:

- How solid and effective is our technology infrastructure?

- How secure is our technology infrastructure?

- What is the structure of the IT Group? Is it internal, outsourced?

- How effective is it?

- How secure is the IT team?

- How safe is it in terms of redundancy and cross-training?

c. Data:

- What are the primary data repositories and content?

- How relevant, comprehensive, and accurate are they?

- How secure is our data?

- How accessible, extractable, and integratable is our data?

Work Processes:

What work processes are involved with the key areas of the business? Here are questions for each:

1. On a scale from 1 to 10, how effective are each of these processes?

2. Are the processes repeatable and measurable?

3. Are they well-documented?

4. Can we create metrics to track our performance relative to each process?

Here are some of key process areas you should consider:

1. Customer Experience:

    a. What discrete encounters and steps do clients participate in?

        1) On their own

        2) In conjunction with your staff

        3) In the background but with their knowledge

        4) In the background without their knowledge

2. Employee Experience:

    a. What discrete encounters and steps do employees participate in?

3. Marketing and Business Development:

    a. Branding and identity

    b. Content creation and dissemination

    c. Search, paid and organic SEO

    d. Website development and maintenance

    e. Outreach and direct sales

    f. Digital ads

    g. Social media

    h. Traditional media

    i. Public relations

4. Manufacturing and assembly

5. Service delivery

6. Recruiting, hiring, and onboarding

6. Education, training, and mentoring

7. Finance and accounting

8. Legal and compliance

9. Strategic planning

ACKNOWLEDGMENTS

T his is my first book, and I'm going to follow a pattern I've noticed from many first-time authors, thanking *so many people*. I hate to drag you through it all, but there is a story here, the story of someone who had the immense good fortune of learning from kind, generous, and brilliant people, folks who helped him progress, sometimes on hands-and-knees, from Point A to Point B, and beyond.

Throughout my career, I have been blessed by wonderful business partners who have taught me, pushed me, and carried so much of the load. It all started with Chuck Blethen, who told me I could become an entrepreneur, then encouraged me to launch Merchantile International in 1983, one month after Kim and I got married. This presented the opportunity to partner with Larry Seifert and Carl Rahn, the founders of SR-1 Aviation. Then came Glenn DeKraker, who invented Aim21 and invited me to help him build it. After that, Michael Berneis, David Hessekiel, Steve White, and Mark LeBlanc worked hard with me to bring Tailwind.com to life. When we sold Aim21 and Tailwind, Jim Vose, a board member of both, asked me to join him at Pemigewasset Partners, opening the door to the worlds of family offices and investment management. After that, the

Corning and Long families asked me to lead and scale Springcreek Advisors. A few years later, Steve Hohenrieder and I launched Featherstone Holdings, then Edward Baker joined us, followed by Clyde Fossum, who helped find and acquire Elevated Outcomes. There you have it: thirty-six years in one paragraph.

Today, we have multiple companies. Among them, Featherstone Holdings continues to thrive, thanks to strong collaboration with Sydney Isle and Laurel Jensen. Sydney Isle, Jason Van Winkle, Joe Van Winkle, Rob Dean and I are building Jump Creek Partners and Recovery help, and we also launched the Sababa Health Group, with Scott and Glenn Primack, Deborah Biggs, and Dan McCormick. A few compelling concepts are incubating as well. We're launching the 9th Group along with Colby Wilcock and Amber and Roy Christiansen, and we are hard at work with Eric Stats to bring the Global Family Group to life. Behind these business partners are hundreds of employees, colleagues, advisors, classmates, and investors, all of whom taught me so many things. Then there are teachers, mentors, and authors, too numerous to mention. And in many ways, most of all, our customers and clients, who are ultimately responsible for this story.

Ever since I became aware of family business through my grandfather, I have been drawn to the challenges of family dynamics and abundance. However, until I met Jay Hughes, Fredda Herz Brown, and Dennis Jaffe, I had no idea that there was an entire profession devoted to this. These people opened a new world for me, then an army of friends, including Paul Perez, Lee Hausner, Fran Lotery, Charlie Grace, Brian Hughes, Scott Budge, Mariann Mihailidis, and Kristi Kuechler filled in many of the blanks. Wonderful organizations, such as the Family Office Exchange, founded by Sara Hamilton, and IPI, founded by Charlotte Beyer, welcomed me into a vibrant industry, dedicated to helping families flourish together across multiple generations. Today, John A. Warnick and my other collaborators at PPI are pushing the boundaries of my understanding, and my new friends at AFHE (Attorneys for Family Held Enterprises), and FFI (The Family Firm Institute) are doing the same.

My next frontier has been to learn how to write. Betty Heller opened that Pandora's Box, encouraging me, literally giving me the courage, to consider it, long ago. Lucy Hedrick helped too, and then my dear friends Warren Musser and Shirzad Chamine led the way by producing wonderful books of their own for me to emulate. I also want to mention my generous friend Nancy Kamei, who nudged me, sometimes gently, sometimes not, back onto my iconoclastic path multiple times.

The first readers of this manuscript were also gentle, thank goodness, and so insightful. Special thanks to them. Many of their names appear elsewhere, in these paragraphs. Then my friends, teachers and taskmasters at Indie Books International, Henry DeVries, Devin DeVries, and Denise Montgomery, helped me shape the ideas into what you see today.

I hope it will come as no surprise to you that by far the most important aspect of my life is my family. Kim comes first, of course, my wife, best friend, and biggest investor. Then our boys, Tucker and Brooks, of whom I am so proud. Our Mom Eva, and Jerry, our Dad. Wendy, Craig, and Josh, my sister and brothers, along with spouses Bill, Kelly, and Kayla, who keep them on the straight-and-narrow path. Grandparents, aunts, uncles, and others, including Polly, Betty and Warren, and Dianne. Then Fisher cousins, especially Janet and Kyle, Erin and Brock, and Jordan. Goodroe family also, far away but important and always in our hearts. I am so grateful to my in-laws, the Millers and their spouses, who welcomed me so long ago, Connie and Doran, Faye, Sue and Blaire, David, and Janet and Chad. Nieces and nephews in wonderful abundance, and friends too, dear friends who have become like family over the years.

It hasn't been easy for any of you, but it has been a terrific ride for me, and I thank you, each one. Even if you're not specifically mentioned here, I acknowledge your gifts. I know we wouldn't have gotten here without you, and I am deeply grateful.

About The Author

Brad Fisher works with entrepreneurial families who want to thrive together across multiple generations, focusing upon transforming and scaling their companies. He is the co-founder and managing partner of Featherstone Holdings.

Brad has devoted most of his professional career to entrepreneurship and family business abundance. Most recently, he led the acquisition of Elevated Billing Solutions, LLC and Recovery Help, LLC in Salt Lake City. While serving as CEO of those companies, Brad developed a passion for the behavioral health sector.

Prior to Featherstone, Brad served as the CEO and chief investment officer of Springcreek Advisors LLC, a California-based multi-family office, and he previously served as a general partner and the Chief Operating Officer for Pemigewasset Capital, a Connecticut-based family office and hedge fund.

Brad built multiple ventures during his early career, including Aim 21, Incorporated, a software company that developed enterprise multimedia database systems for advertising agencies and their clients. After selling Aim 21 to Reuters in 1997, he founded Tailwind, Incorporated, an online resource center for entrepreneurs and small business owners. The American Towns Network acquired Tailwind in 2001.

Brad Fisher received an MBA from Stanford University and a BS in Economics from the University of Minnesota. He is or has been a board member or Trustee of many companies and non-profit institutions, including Saybrook University, Perrot Memorial Library, ARI of Connecticut, and the Purposeful Planning Institute.

He lives in Salt Lake City, Utah with his wife Kim. Together, they have two sons, Tucker and Brooks.

Made in the USA
Monee, IL
18 January 2021

55890071R00116